WordPress Top Plugins

Find and install the best plugins for generating
and sharing content, building communities,
and generating revenue

Brandon Corbin

BIRMINGHAM - MUMBAI

WordPress Top Plugins

First published: September 2010

Production Reference: 1150910

Published by Packt Publishing Ltd.
32 Lincoln Road
Olton
Birmingham, B27 6PA, UK.

ISBN 978-1-849511-40-7

www.packtpub.com

Cover Image by John Quick (john.m.quick@gmail.com)

Credits

Author
Brandon Corbin

Reviewer
M. Liz Allyn

Acquisition Editor
Usha Iyer

Development Editor
Mayuri Kokate

Technical Editors
Rupal Pravin Joshi
Manasi Poonthottam

Copy Editor
Leonard D'Silva

Indexer
Hemangini Bari

Editorial Team Leader
Aanchal Kumar

Project Team Leader
Priya Mukherjee

Project Coordinator
Vincila Colaco

Proofreader
Aaron Nash

Production Coordinator
Shantanu Zagade

Cover Work
Shantanu Zagade

About the Author

Brandon Corbin is an accomplished web enthusiast with a background in advertising, and has used his knowledge of design and marketing to create websites for many of the Fortune 500. For more than a decade, he has applied his passions to several industries — including radio, real estate, pharmaceuticals, recruiting, and e-Commerce — with an obsessive attention to creating a smooth user experience.

I would like to thank my wonderful wife Emily and my awesome children — Maddy and Ethan, all of whom put up with my absence during the writing of this book. You guys mean the world to me.

About the Reviewer

M. Liz Allyn has been interested in computers since her high school days, and minored in Computer Science and Math while finishing her BS in Chemistry. After earning a Master of Science in Analytical Chemistry, she worked as a development scientist, group leader, and senior quality assurance officer. These real jobs in the chemical and pharmaceutical industries taught her that she hated cubicles.

To Liz, the fun part was teaching the technicians and working in the laboratories with the instrumentation. Her most interesting lab project was programming a robot in a pharmaceutical lab to prepare samples for chemical analysis. Sample preparation time was reduced by 75 percent, which allowed the technicians to attend to other tasks.

In between teaching assignments Liz taught herself html, became a certified webmaster, and learned to use PHP and MySQL in developing websites. She has been blogging with WordPress for four years now.

Among a few websites that she keeps active Liz likes to share tips about WordPress and the underlying HTML, CSS, PHP, and MySQL with her readers at `computeraxe.com`. When she's not helping clients deal with their website or database issues, Liz enjoys writing about plants and sharing pictures of nature at her WordPress blog, `wildeherb.com`.

Table of Contents

Preface

WordPress has thousands of plugins available—most of them don't work as advertised, are out dated, or simply don't work. Wordpress Top Plugins takes you through the process of finding the very best plugins to build a powerful and engaging website or blog.

With access to over 10,000 plugins, finding the ones that actually work as advertised is becoming exceedingly difficult and time consuming. Wordpress Top Plugins removes this time-consuming act by delivering only the best free plugins available on WordPress today.

Each chapter tackles common objectives most websites need to achieve, such as: building a community, sharing content, working with multiple authors, and securing your website. With exact search terms, screenshots, and complexity levels, you'll find exactly what you need to quickly install and setup each of the plugins that fits your technical skills.

What this book covers

Chapter 1, Plugin Basics covers the basics in finding, choosing, and installing plugins on your WordPress powered blog.

Chapter 2, Generating Content will expose the top plugins for dynamically creating content on your blog.

Chapter 3, Sharing Content will help you turn your blog in to a content sharing machine by making it easy for your readers and yourself to promote your blogs content across the entire social web.

Chapter 4, Style and Function covers the best WordPress plugins for increasing your blog's usability, beauty, and fun.

Chapter 5, Building a Community with BuddyPress shows you, step by step, how to turn your blog into a full blown social network.

Chapter 6, Generate Revenue will show you the best plugins for creating on-going automated revenue for your website.

Chapter 7, Working with Multiple Authors highlights the best plugins for websites with multiple writers.

Chapter 8, Security and Maintenance covers plugins that help maintain a healthy and secure WordPress blog.

Chapter 9, Power Admin covers the plugins that will turn you in to a WordPress administrating juggernaut.

Chapter 10, Time for Action covers some of the best external resources for continuing your WordPress education.

What you need for this book

WordPress 2.8 or higher.

Who this book is for

Regardless if this is your first-time working with WordPress, or you're a seasoned WordPress coding ninja — WordPress Top Plugins will walk you through finding and installing the best plugins for generating and sharing content, building communities and reader base, and generating real advertising revenue.

Conventions

In this book, you will find a number of styles of text that distinguish between different kinds of information. Here are some examples of these styles, and an explanation of their meaning.

Code words in text are shown as follows: "You can also include `[blogurl]`, `[blogtitle]`, and `[backtime]`; each will be replaced with the actual information when a user visits the site."

A block of code is set as follows:

```
<div style="text-align:center;
  margin:5px;
  padding:5px;
  border-bottom:solid 1px #CCCCCC;">
  <a href="http://twitter.com/[YOUR-TWITTER-USERNAME]">
    Do you follow me on twitter?
  </a>
</div>
```

New terms and **important words** are shown in bold. Words that you see on the screen, in menus or dialog boxes for example, appear in the text like this: "clicking the **Next** button moves you to the next screen".

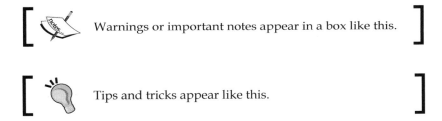

> Warnings or important notes appear in a box like this.

> Tips and tricks appear like this.

Reader feedback

Feedback from our readers is always welcome. Let us know what you think about this book—what you liked or may have disliked. Reader feedback is important for us to develop titles that you really get the most out of.

To send us general feedback, simply send an e-mail to feedback@packtpub.com, and mention the book title via the subject of your message.

If there is a book that you need and would like to see us publish, please send us a note in the **SUGGEST A TITLE** form on www.packtpub.com or e-mail suggest@packtpub.com.

If there is a topic that you have expertise in and you are interested in either writing or contributing to a book, see our author guide on www.packtpub.com/authors.

Customer support

Now that you are the proud owner of a Packt book, we have a number of things to help you to get the most from your purchase.

Downloading the example code for this book

You can download the example code files for all Packt books you have purchased from your account at http://www.PacktPub.com. If you purchased this book elsewhere, you can visit http://www.PacktPub.com/support and register to have the files e-mailed directly to you.

Errata

Although we have taken every care to ensure the accuracy of our content, mistakes do happen. If you find a mistake in one of our books—maybe a mistake in the text or the code—we would be grateful if you would report this to us. By doing so, you can save other readers from frustration and help us improve subsequent versions of this book. If you find any errata, please report them by visiting http://www.packtpub.com/support, selecting your book, clicking on the **errata submission form** link, and entering the details of your errata. Once your errata are verified, your submission will be accepted and the errata will be uploaded on our website, or added to any list of existing errata, under the Errata section of that title. Any existing errata can be viewed by selecting your title from http://www.packtpub.com/support.

Piracy

Piracy of copyright material on the Internet is an ongoing problem across all media. At Packt, we take the protection of our copyright and licenses very seriously. If you come across any illegal copies of our works, in any form, on the Internet, please provide us with the location address or website name immediately so that we can pursue a remedy.

Please contact us at copyright@packtpub.com with a link to the suspected pirated material.

We appreciate your help in protecting our authors, and our ability to bring you valuable content.

Questions

You can contact us at questions@packtpub.com if you are having a problem with any aspect of the book, and we will do our best to address it.

1
Plugin Basics

There is literally a plugin for almost anything you want to achieve in WordPress. A quick glance at the WordPress Plugin Directory will show you just how many options are available. Admin, Ajax, Comments, Google, Posts, Sidebar, Twitter, and Widgets are all so very well represented that finding the right one can be a full-time gig. Twitter alone has over 200 plugins dedicated to pulling, pushing, and searching through its masses of data. However, before we can auto-tweet a post, or dynamically interleave links to Amazon products, we have to comprehend how a plugin works, and more importantly, how to install and activate them on our blog.

Every plugin is written in PHP (an awesome open source programming language) and are usually accompanied by various other internet file types such as CSS, Javascript, XML, images, JSON files, and so on. Thanks to WordPress's open architecture, developers can inject their plugin's code throughout your blog without you having to touch a single line of code, unless, of course, you want to.

In this chapter, we cover the following:

- Installing plugins
- How plugins work
- Troubleshooting plugins

Safety first

It's very much imperative to understand that plugins have the ability to affect virtually every part of your blog. If a plugin developer was feeling decidedly evil, he/she could create mayhem to your website with a few tiny lines of code. Make sure you trust the recommending source that's promoting a plugin *before you install it.*

I personally recommend and reference almost exclusively throughout this book http://Wordpress.org/extend/plugins, the official Wordpress.org Plugin Directory. This self-policing community often provides very valuable and detailed pros and cons for almost every plugin, with the ability to sort by popularity, rank, and date released.

Automatic install versus manual install

WordPress offers two main methods to install a plugin. One is WordPress' own baked-in Plugin Installer (results may vary) and the other is the manual method using SFTP or FTP. WordPress's automatic install makes life significantly easier, depending on your webhosting provider, however it might not be available for your hosting package. If this is the case, and your site doesn't support automatic install, you can still manually install plugins using FTP.

Honestly, if your host doesn't support automatic installation, you should seriously consider changing web hosts. The ability to automatically install WordPress updates, plugin updates, and new plugins is one of the reasons WordPress is great; the process is hard enough without letting things become outdated.

Automatic plugin installation

Out of the box, WordPress comes with its own plugin app store, which allows you to search through a huge library of free plugins. To access WordPress's built-in plugin browser, click **Add New** under the Plugins menu. Once inside the plugin app store, you have the option to either search by keyword or name, browse by popular tags, or see the newest plugins added.

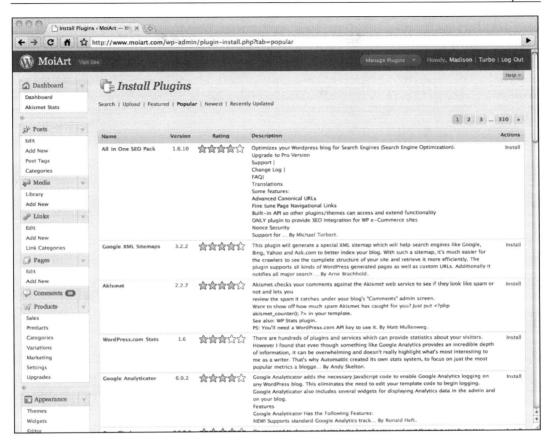

After you search or browse by a tag, you will be presented with a list of plugins that are available for you to install from WordPress's Plugin Directory. Each will list its version number (the later the version, the more stable, usually), a community rating, a more detailed description, and an `Install` link.

Now is a good time to remember that you are dealing with FREE software; what you are about to install will most likely offer NO guarantees or warrantees. Never forget that a plugin runs server-side code on your website, which means that a plugin can access your database(s), can read, write, and delete files, and even send e-mails from your domain.

 Please read the reviews and listen to what the community has to say about the plugin you are about to install.

If a plugin is rated with 1 star by a lot of the community, it would be wise to keep your distance. But if a plugin has been installed 40,000 times and has a 3+ star rating, it's fair to say that it is trustworthy.

Clicking **Install** on this screen will not actually install the plugin; instead, it will launch a window that provides even more details about the specific plugin.

Plugin detail

The plugin details pop-up window provides you with a deeper look into the plugin you are about to install.

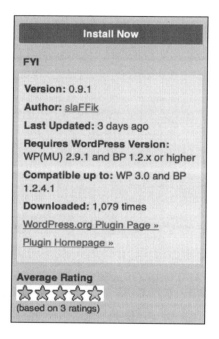

The important areas to pay attention to are as follows:

- The number of downloads shows how popular a plugin is.
- The average rating shows you what the community thinks about the plugin.
- **Last Updated** date tells you if the project is still being actively worked upon.
- **Compatible up to** tells you if the plugin has been tested on your version or not. Keep in mind that a lot of plugins might not have been "tested" with your current version, but will still work.

Many times, plugins require no additional setup or configuration, while others need a bit more tooling around to get running. If the developer provided Installation instructions, make sure to look them over to ensure that you're not getting in over your head. If you are happy with what you see, click the big red **Install Now** button.

Downloading, unpacking, installing

If, after clicking the **Install Now** button, you make it through all of the steps and see **Activate Plugin**, you're in for a treat! Congratulations, your web host supports the Automatic Install of WordPress.

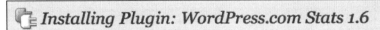

Installing Plugin: WordPress.com Stats 1.6

Downloading install package from http://downloads.wordpress.org/plugin/stats.1.6.zip.

Unpacking the package.

Installing the plugin.

Successfully installed the plugin **WordPress.com Stats 1.6**.

Actions: Activate Plugin | Return to Plugin Installer

Activating the plugin

While you have installed the plugin, you aren't done yet! We still need to activate it.

Once you click **Activate Plugin**, WordPress will go through the process of turning the plugin on. Depending on what the plugin does, this process could include creating new database tables or setting up new folders and files.

Once activated, you still might be required to provide more information before the plugin can run properly. For example, if you're installing Alex King's Twitter Tools plugin, you'll need to provide your Twitter credentials before it can do any of its magic.

Connection Information required

If, when you click **Install Now**, you see the **Connection Information** form, like the image in the next screenshot, then we have a little more work to do before we can start installing plugins automatically. However, you still have a chance to have "Automatic Install" if your hosting-provider allows it. Follow the next few steps to see if it's still a possibility. Don't worry if the next steps fail; we will still be able to install plugins quickly, just not as quickly as the "Automatic Install".

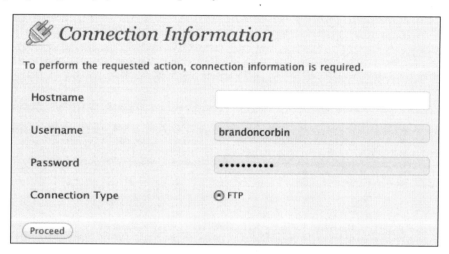

In this window, provide your **Hostname**, which will most likely be just your domain name. For example: `icorbin.com` (minus the http), your FTP username, and its password. Some installations might have FTP and SFTP for the connection type; if SFTP is available and it works when you click proceed, use it.

If your web host doesn't support this method, then we need to attack the problem without WordPress and instead use our own FTP client.

Manual installation

If you find that the Automatic Install feature isn't compatible with your web-hosting provider, then manual installation is the next best option. In this section, we will cover how to do it on both a Mac and PC.

At the highest level, manually installing a plugin will require you to connect to your web server, locate the WordPress plugins directory, and transfer a plugin that you have downloaded to your computer using either FTP or SFTP. Once you connect to your web server, you will need to locate your WordPress Plugin folder, which will most likely be in `wp-content/plugins`.

Manually installing a plugin with a Mac

If you do not currently have an FTP/SFTP application on your Mac, then I highly recommend Cyberduck, the best free FTP/SFTP client available for the Mac. You can download a free copy of Cyberduck from `http://cyberduck.ch/`.

After launching the **Open Connection**, located in the upper-right–hand side of the Applications window, the following screenshot will ask for the specifics on connecting to your website. This information can all be usually found in your web host's control panel or the initial setup e-mail you received when you created your hosting account.

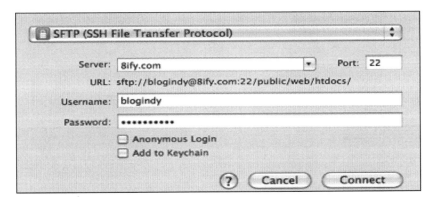

- **Connection Type**: FTP, SFTP FTP-SSL. Which connection you should use depends on what your web-hosting provider supports. Almost all web hosts offer the less secure FTP protocol, but if you can, I would suggest connecting with SFTP (Secure FTP).
- **Server**: the domain name or IP address of your website.
- **Username**: your FTP account username.
- **Password**: your FTP account password.

Click **Connect**.

If everything connects properly, you should see a list of files that exist on your website.

Browse to your plugin directory located at `wp-content/plugins`. This folder is where we will be putting any new plugin we want to install.

To save time, you can create a bookmark in Cyberduck, and save it on your desktop or Dock so you are only a click away from your plugin folder. To create a bookmark, select **New Bookmark** from Cyberduck's **Action** drop-down menu.

Transferring a plugin

Once you have downloaded the plugin to your computer, you will need to move it over to your website. To do this, we will move the plugin (most likely a .ZIP archive) to your website's FTP directory. Using Cyberduck, we will extract the ZIP file on the server. Extracting archives on the server can save significant time, as we are only uploading one file opposed to the hundreds some plugins can contain.

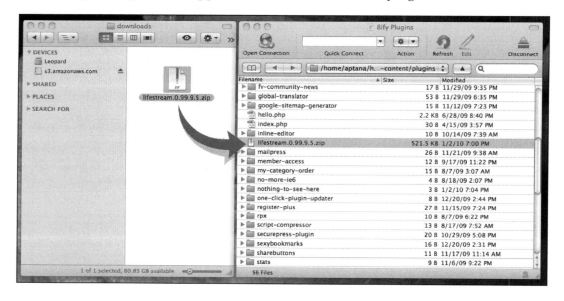

Now that we have the plugin's ZIP archive in the plugins directory, we need to expand it or unzip it. Cyberduck offers a super quick way for us to expand archived files like ZIP, TAR, and Gzip by right-clicking on your plugin and selecting **Expand Archive**.

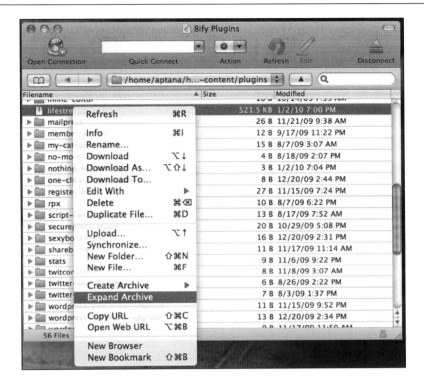

Manually installing a plugin on Windows

For Windows users, I suggest the open source application called WinSCP—this great utility will allow you to connect to your server by FTP, SFTP, and FTP-SSL. To download WinSCP, visit http://winscp.net.

Once you have downloaded and installed `WinSCP`, launch the application, and you will be presented with the following screenshot:

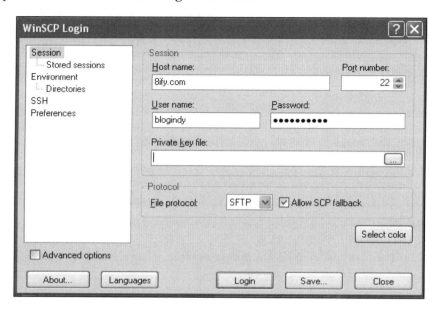

- **Host Name**: The domain name or IP address of your website
- **Port number**: Leave this field as it is, as it will be set when we select a protocol in the next couple of steps
- **Username**: Your FTP account's username
- **Password**: Your FTP account's password

Next click **Login**.

If everything connects properly, you should see the following screenshot, which will contain all of the files that exist on your website, in a similar fashion that Windows Explorer does.

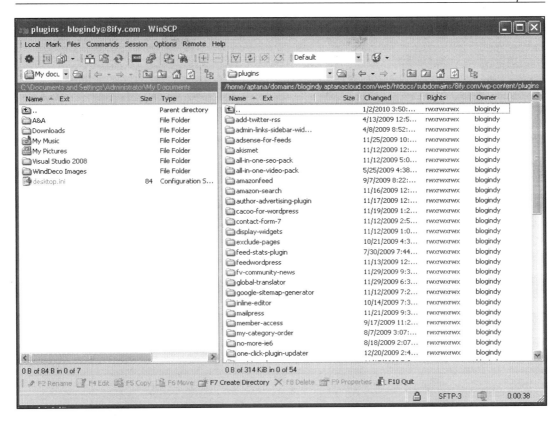

Most website providers keep all of the website files in a specific directory; our goal is to find this folder and proceed to `wp-content/plugins`. If you do not see `wp-content`, then look for a folder like `htdocs`, `httpdocs`, or `www`. Once you locate this folder, inside you should find the folders and files that make up your WordPress installation.

Once inside the plugins folder, we want to create a bookmark so that we can access this folder super quickly next time.

Creating a bookmark with WinSCP

Bookmarks are a super-easy way to connect to your server without having to remember the username, password, and path to your plugins directory. Once you have clicked your way to your plugins directory (located at `wp-content/plugins/`), click the **Remote** menu item, and select **Add Bookmark**, or you can simply click *Ctrl+B*.

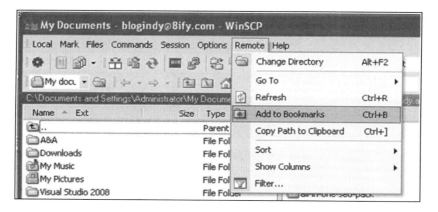

Transferring a plugin to your blog

Once you have downloaded a plugin to your desktop, you will simply drag the unzipped folder directly into the `wp-content/plugins` directory.

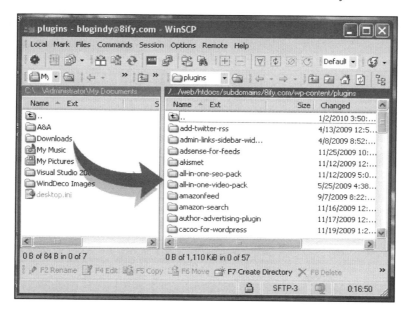

Activating your plugin

Now that we have installed the plugin on the server, either by using Cyberduck on the Mac, WinSCP on Windows, or old school SSH, we still have one more step to go, namely, to activate the plugin.

To activate our plugin, we will first need to visit our plugin browser by expanding the "Appearance" tab and clicking on "Plugins". The plugin browser will display all of the plugins that are currently installed—inactive plugins have a light gray background while active plugins are denoted with a white background.

Once you have located the plugin you just installed, click the "Active Plugin" link. WordPress will now go through the steps needed to get that plugin ready and roaring.

Once your plugin has been activated, you will need to determine if there are any additional steps required to complete the plugin setup. Some of the more complex plugins might require you to provide additional information or might need some special code added to your WordPress theme files. It all really depends on the plugin that you are installing. If you found the plugin through the WordPress directory, then you will most likely find instructions that will tell you exactly the steps you will need to take.

Finding a plugin's settings

Most plugins have some sort of "settings"; other common names include "configuration" or "options"—each developer has their own special place to include this illusive panel. Because each plugin can stick its options in a ton of different spots throughout the WordPress administrator's navigation, I will make sure to tell you specifically where this page is for each of the plugins covered in this book. For those plugins you install without the guidance of this book, here are a few spots to look.

- **Top Navigation | Settings**
- **Top Navigation | Plugins**
- **Top Navigation | Tools**

How plugins work

WordPress has designated areas that developers can leverage within their plugin; these areas are rightfully named **Hooks**. Currently, the two types of hooks available are Actions and Filters.

An **Action** is a hook that's triggered during common blogging events such as creating a post or deleting a comment. For example, the `publish_post` action is triggered whenever a post is finally published. Similarly, the `wp_insert_comment` is fired each time a website visitor leaves a comment.

A **Filter**, like an Action, is a hook that plugin developers use to modify various types of data before it's added to your database or displaying it to the end user. For example, the `the_content` filter is applied whenever your blog renders a "Posts" content. The `content_save_pre` filter is applied right before a blog post's body content is saved to a database.

You can learn more about Actions, Filters, and WordPress Plugins in general at:

- Plugin API: `http://codex.Wordpress.org/Plugin_API`
- Writing a Plugin: `http://codex.Wordpress.org/Writing_a_Plugin`
- Actions: `http://codex.Wordpress.org/Plugin_API/Action_Reference`
- Plugin Coding Standards: `http://codex.Wordpress.org/WordPress_Coding_Standards`

Managing plugins

WordPress provides a wonderful built-in plugin manager for installing, activating, deactivating, and editing plugins. You will be spending a good majority of your time in the plugin manager. The sooner you become comfortable with it, the better.

- **Add New Plugin button** lets you browse quickly all of the available plugins from WordPress's Plugin Directory directly from your Administrator section.
- **The Search for Plugins** input box will allow you to quickly filter through all of the plugins you currently have installed.
- Organize your currently installed plugins by clicking on any of the filter links like **Active, Inactive**, and **Upgrade Available**.
- **Out-of-Date** plugins are signified by the presence of the yellow bar that states "There is a new version of [PLUGIN NAME] followed by an Upgrade Automatically link".

Keeping your plugins up-to-date

With WordPress's "automatic-updates", keeping all of your plugins up-to-date is a breeze. With a quick glance at your plugin manager, you'll know precisely which plugins need to be updated. A click on the `Upgrade Automatically` link performs all of the necessary actions to download, back up, and install the newest version of the plugin.

Out-of-date plugins are highlighted along with a message that says "There is a new version of Plugin Name available". In order to keep your blog running smoothly and securely, make sure that you keep your plugins up-to-date.

Learn by tinkering

Seeing how a developer handles a specific problem, how he/she then tries to break it, and then fixes it, is good way to learn how to program in PHP. Moreover, thanks to WordPress's built-in fail-safes—breaking a plugin will, most likely, not break your website.

WordPress plugin API

WordPress's plugin API at `http://codex.Wordpress.org/Plugin_API` contains all of the WordPress-specific tags, functions, and insights in to making and modifying plugins.

PHP references

As mentioned before, each plugin is written in PHP, which means that a plugin has access to every PHP function that exists—all 700 of them. To learn more about PHP and all of the cool stuff that you can do with it, head over to the PHP manual at `http://php.net`.

CSS

Cascading Style Sheets is a standard language for defining the look and feel of text and other elements on a web page. CSS is what you will use to "style" a plugin beyond its original design. You can learn more about CSS from any of these great resources at `http://delicious.com/popular/css`.

JavaScript

JavaScript is another very popular programming language that runs on your browser—opposed to the server-side nature of PHP. JavaScript allows you to make changes to virtually any part of your website without having to tinker with PHP. For more information about JavaScript, check out `http://delicious.com/popular/javascript`.

Troubleshooting plugins

- Often, you will notice that problems arise for plugins after a large update to the entire WordPress platform. In any case, the following are a few tips to try if you encounter any problems getting your plugins to run. **My plugin stops working after an update**—Check the Plugin's website (listed in the Plugin Browser) to see if any known issues exist.

- **I can't find the plugin in my Plugin Browser**—Make sure you uploaded it to the correct folder: `wp-content/plugins`.

- **Check the plugin's version compatibility**—There is a chance that the plugin just won't work with a new version of WordPress; if this is the case, hopefully, the developer will release an update soon.

- **My plugin says I don't have permission to X folder**—Permissions are settings on files and folders that either allow or disallow a user to write to them. You can learn more about setting permissions at `http://codex.Wordpress.org/Changing_File_Permissions`.

- **My plugin should be showing X on my post, but it's not**—Many times, a plugin requires you to place a custom tag within your post to "trigger" the plugin; read the plugin's installation documentation.

- **I can't find the answer on the plugins' website**—A quick google search for "problems installing [PLUGIN NAME] on WordPress" will lead you to an answer. You can also check the forum link on the plugin's homepage in the plugin directory at `http://Wordpress.org/extend/plugins`.

- **Google didn't give me the answer I was looking for**—Search WordPress's plugin directory for a different plugin.

□ Plugin	Description
Akismet	Akismet checks your comments against the Akismet web service to see if they look like spam or not. You need a WordPress.com API key to use it. You can review the spam it catches under "Comments." To show off your Akismet stats just put `<?php akismet_counter(); ?>` in your template. See also: WP Stats plugin.
□ Deactivate | Edit	Version 2.2.7 | By Matt Mullenweg | Visit plugin site
All in One SEO Pack	Out-of-the-box SEO for your Wordpress blog. Options configuration panel | Donate | Support | Amazon Wishlist
□ Deactivate | Edit	Version 1.6.5 | By Michael Torbert | Visit plugin site

There is a new version of All in One SEO Pack available. View version 1.6.10 Details **or** upgrade automatically.

□ WordPress.com Stats	Tracks views, post/page views, referre... ...ess.com API key.
Deactivate | Edit	Version 1.6 | By Andy Skelton | Visit plugin site
□ WP Shopping Cart	A plugin that provides a WordPress Shopping Cart. Contact Instinct Entertainment for support.
Deactivate | Edit	Version 3.7.4 | By Instinct Entertainment | Visit plugin site

There is a new version of WP Shopping Cart available. View version 3.7.5.3 Details **or** upgrade automatically.

□ Plugin	Description

Time to Update.

Editing plugins

If you are a power user or someone who likes to get their hands dirty, you will love the Plugin Editor! This little feature allows you to see the raw source of the plugin, and even make changes to it (if you have set the plugins folder to writable). To learn more about file and folder permissions, head over to `http://codex.Wordpress.org/Changing_File_Permissions`.

By clicking through **Plugins | Plugin Editor**, you will be presented with the code for the main plugin file. If your plugin folder is writable, you will be able to make changes and click **Save**. WordPress has safeguards in place to ensure that if you happen to make a mistake with the plugin, that it automatically becomes deactivated. If, at any point, you mangle a plugin to the point where you can no longer fix it, simply delete the plugin and reinstall it.

Summary

In this chapter, we covered how to use the Automatic Installation of plugins and how to install plugins manually using SFTP and FTP for both Macs and PCs. I hope you also learned that while plugins can rock your world, they can also be extremely dangerous and should always be handled with care.

The next chapter will focus on plugins that allow you to create content, improve WordPress's search, greet your visitors with personalized messages, and much more.

2
Generating Content

A blog without content is like a dinner plate with no food. And while WordPress makes it easy to generate content for your blog, out of the box, it's an empty canvas waiting to be filled with dazzling content.

In this chapter, we cover the following:

- Adding ratings to your blog posts
- Automatically creating links to similar blog posts
- Easily including videos from YouTube, Vimeo, and many more
- Creating personalized greetings for your visitors
- Creating slideshows
- Building forms
- Improving WordPress's search
- Automatically pulling content from your other websites

GD Star Rating

By Milan Petrovic (`http://dev4press.com/`)

- **Why it's awesome**: Quickly adds ratings and ranking to your blog posts
- **Why it was picked**: Super easy to get running, offers lots of customizations

- **Manual Install URL**:
  `http://wordpress.org/extend/plugins/gd-star-rating/`

- **Automatic Install search term**: GD Star Rating
- **Geek level**: Newbie
- **Configuration location**: Top Navigation | GD Star Rating
- **Used in**: Posts, comments, pages

If you want to know what your readers like, then you need to allow them to quickly rate your individual posts and rank other readers' comments; **GD Star Rating** does exactly this. Don't be fooled by its deceptively simple outer shell. Those rating stars are backed by a massive administrative area that allows you to customize virtually every aspect of how a user rates your blog's content. For example, you can change how the stars look, how many times to allow users to vote, where to display ratings, and much, much more. In addition to being crazily customizable, GD Star Rating also offers awesome analytics on who's rating what, which items are popular, and virtually any other data point you could imagine.

Fixing the default ratings

Out of the box, GD Star Rating will include both a 10 Star Rating bar and a Thumbs Up/Thumbs Down ranking scale. Obviously, a post doesn't need both, and 10 Star Rating will work just fine for all of our blog posts. The Thumbs Up/Thumbs Down will be great for our comments.

[To access GD Star Rating's main settings, visit **GD Star Rating | Settings**.]

Turning off Thumbs Up/Thumbs Down on posts

Uncheck the checkbox next to **For Individual Posts** and **For Individual Pages**.

Turning off Star Ratings on comments

Uncheck the checkbox next to **For Comments for Posts** and **For Comments for Pages**.

Better Tag Cloud

By Nicolas Kuttler (http://www.nkuttler.de/)

- **Why it's awesome**: It's not really awesome, just wonderfully practical and create a nicely customizable TagCloud

- **Why it was picked**: Updated often, flexibility of placement, color customizations

» design (1) » love (1) » **magic** (2) »
mobile (2) » **php** (2) » **Science** (2) » Sky (1)
» software (1) » **Space** (2) » telescopes (1) »
wake (1) » **wordpress** (4)

- **Manual Install URL**: http://wordpress.org/extend/plugins/nktagcloud/

- **Automatic Install search term**: Better Tag Cloud

- **Geek level**: Newbie

- **Configuration location**: **Settings | Better Tag Cloud**

- **Used in**: Posts, pages, widgets

The Tag Cloud widget that comes with WordPress is very simple. Luckily, Nicolas Kuttler took the initiative to create a wonderful replacement. Not only does **Better Tag Cloud** give you a new widget, it also lets you include your tag cloud in posts and pages.

 Use the shortcode [nktagcloud] to include *Better Tag Cloud* in a post or page.

Yet Another Related Posts Plugin (YARPP)

By Michael Yoshitaka Erlewine (`http://mitcho.com/`)

- **Why it's awesome**: Search engine optimization and increasing average time on site for you visitors
- **Why it was picked**: Accuracy of the relation algorithm

Related posts:

Free Christmas Stock Photos (11.491)   The Christmas is coming and Christmas decorations are...

Less Than Free (9.246) VC Bill Gurley has up an insightful piece on the...

Designing CSS Buttons: Techniques and Resources (8.423) Buttons, whatever their purpose..

The Post Transaction Marketing Wall Of Shame (8.262) Later today Senator Rockefeller is holding a...

Win a Free Book, 'CSS Mastery: Advanced Web Standards Solutions' *(8.213)* ...

Related posts brought to you by *Yet Another Related Posts Plugin.*

- **Manual Install URL**: `http://wordpress.org/extend/plugins/yet-another-related-posts-plugin/`
- **Automatic Install search term**: YARPP
- **Geek level**: Newbie
- **Configuration location**: **Settings | Related Posts (YARPP)**
- **Used in**: Posts

Yet Another Related Posts Plugin (YARPP) helps your readers and the search engine bots to find other posts on your website that are similar to the one they are currently reading.

Once installed and activated, the YARPP plugin is virtually done. Check out one of your blog posts, and see if you like the results. Below the article will be a list of similar posts to the one you're reading. While out of the box YARPP will satisfy 80 percent of the people, you should check out the YARPP settings, as it offers a ton of configuration options.

My Page Order

By Andrew Charlton (`http://www.geekyweekly.com/`)

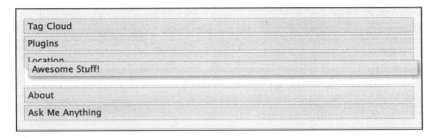

- **Manual Install URL**:
  `http://wordpress.org/extend/plugins/my-page-order/`
- **Automatic Install search term**: My Page Order
- **Geek level**: Newbie
- **Configuration location: Pages | My Page Order**
- **Used in**: Navigation

My Page Order, by Andrew Charlton, allows you to reorder your WordPress pages using a super simple drag-and-drop interface.

Get Recent Comments

By Krischan Jodies (`http://jodies.de`)

- **Why it's awesome**: Helps search engine optimization and the visitors know what content is the most talked about
- **Why it was picked**: Simplicity and search engine optimization

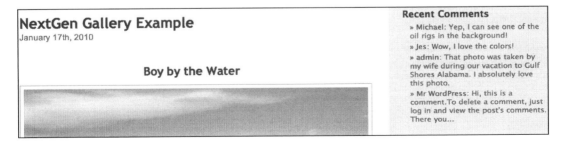

- **Manual Install URL**:
  http://wordpress.org/extend/plugins/get-recent-comments/
- **Automatic Install search term**: Get Recent Comments
- **Geek level**: Newbie
- **Configuration location**: **Settings | Recent Comments**
- **Used in**: Widgets, templates

The default **Recent Comments** widget in WordPress is shockingly incomplete; luckily, Krischan Jodies spent his personal time to build a proper Recent Comments widget. Once activated, you will need to visit **Appearance | Widgets**. A new **Recent Comments** widget will be available to drag to your sidebar. Out of the box, the plugin needs no configuration, but Krischan provided a very comprehensive configuration engine that can be accessed through **Settings | Recent Comments**.

The plugin, Recent Comments, also comes with a **Recent Trackback** widget. You might ask "What's a Trackback?"; a Trackback is simply when someone mentions your post or website on their blog or website.

Viper's Video Quicktags

By Alex—also known as Viper007Bond (http://www.viper007bond.com/)

- **Why it's awesome**: Add and embed a video from the most popuplar online source
- **Why it was picked**: Simplicity and number of video services support

- **Manual Install URL**: `http://wordpress.org/extend/plugins/vipers-video-quicktags/`
- **Automatic Install search term**: Vipers Video Quicktags
- **Geek level**: Newbie
- **Configuration location: Settings | Video Quicktags**
- **Used in**: Posts

Embedding videos has never been easier, thanks to **Vipers Video Quicktags**. This plugin removes the need to copy and paste "embed" code from the different video sharing sites into your posts' body. Instead, you click the icon for a specific video site, for example, YouTube. Then all you need to provide is the URL to the video. Viper's Video Quicktag goes to the URL and extracts the embed code automatically.

WP Greet Box

By Thaya Kareeson (`http://omninoggin.com`)

- **Why it's awesome**: It just works, and it offers the user a direct call to action
- **Why it was picked**: Simplicity and customizability

- **Manual Install URL**: `http://wordpress.org/extend/plugins/wp-greet-box/`
- **Automatic Install search term**: WP Greet Box
- **Geek level**: Newbie
- **Configuration location: Settings | WP Greet Box**
- **Used in**: Posts, pages

WP Greet Box allows you to display custom messages to visitors, depending on where they originated from. For example, if a reader comes to your blog from Google Reader, the default message will welcome them as a "Google Reader" and give them the ability to subscribe to your blog's RSS feed. Similarly, when a visitor comes from Twitter, you can welcome the Twitter user with the option of following you on Twitter.

NextGen Gallery

By Alex Rabe (`http://alexrabe.de/`)

- **Why it's awesome**: Produces beautiful slideshows quickly
- **Why it was picked**: Continually updated by the developer and ease of install and use

- **Manual Install URL**:
  `http://wordpress.org/extend/plugins/nextgen-gallery/`
- **Automatic Install search term**: NextGen Gallery
- **Geek level**: Webmaster
- **Configuration location: Top Navigation | Gallery**
- **Used in**: Posts, pages, widgets

Alex Rabe's **NextGen Gallery** is hands down the most popular plugin(by means of total downloads) available for WordPress. NextGen Gallery supports multiple photo galleries, multiple ways to display your photos, and other developers are even creating sub plugins for it! Once installed, you will be able to include your photo albums on both Pages and Posts, as a slideshow (see the following note), image list, or image gallery.

Note: To take advantage of the Flash Slideshow display, you will need to download *JW Image Rotator* from `http://www.longtailvideo.com/players/jw-image-rotator/`. Once downloaded, you will need to put the SWF file in your `wp-content/uploads` directory. JW Image Rotator is released under the Creative Commons license.

Setting up your first gallery

Start off by clicking **Add Gallery | Image** in the Gallery navigation. The screen will display a tabbed interface, allowing you to add a new gallery, upload a ZIP file of multiple images, import an image folder (located on your server), or manually upload an image one at a time.

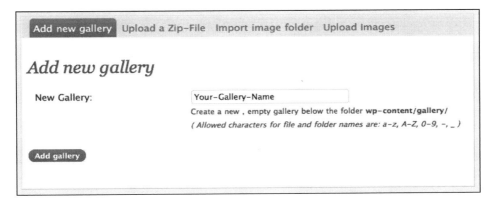

- Give a name to your gallery. For this demonstration, I named mine **Your-Gallery-Name**. Then click **Add Gallery**
- Click the **Upload Images** tab
  - Click **browse** and select your first photo
  - Select which Gallery you would like to put this photo in
  - NOTE: you will always need to select this for each photo you upload
  - Click **Upload Image**
  - Rinse and repeat as needed

Congratulations, you just created your first photo gallery. Now that we have a gallery with photos, let's insert it into a post. The process for adding a gallery to a post is exactly the same as adding it to a page.

Adding your gallery to a post or a page

Once you visit your **Add Post** or **Add Page** area of WordPress, you should notice a new icon available—this is your NextGen Gallery button.

On clicking the newly created button, a new pop-up window will give you the option to select which gallery to include and which method the gallery should be displayed in. Also available from this pop-up window is the option to include an individual photo or an album that contains multiple photo galleries.

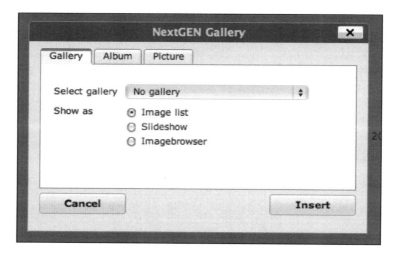

Zemanta

By Thaya Kareeson (http://zemanta.com)

- **Why it's awesome**: Zemanta makes it a snap to have posts with relevant imagery and links
- **Why it was picked**: Auto linking content, creative common images, and related posts from all over the net

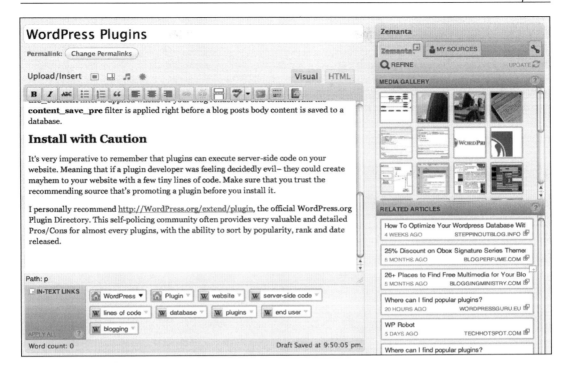

- **Manual Install URL**: http://wordpress.org/extend/plugins/zemanta/
- **Automatic Install search term**: Zemanta
- **Geek level**: Webmaster
- **Configuration location**: Plugins | Zemanta Configuration
- **Used in**: Posts

Zemanta is an awesome plugin that helps you automatically find helpful links, photos, and other online sources that relate directly to the post you're writing. Once installed, you will see a new side-panel when you create or edit a post or page. Once you start typing in the body of your post, Zemanta will automatically scour the web looking for photos and other blog posts that cover similar items.

To use Zemanta, simply start writing a new blog post. Beneath the post, you will find a panel called "IN-TEXT LINKS". As you write, specific keywords will be listed in this panel. These keywords are links to websites that Zemanta found online. Clicking one of these keywords will automatically create a link to the website.

In the side-bar panel, Zemanta includes a panel of related images and a panel of related posts online that relate directly to the content you are producing. Clicking on one of the images Zemanta found will insert the image at the current cursor position.

CForms II

By Oliver Seidel (`http://deliciousdays.com`)

- **Why** it's awesome: Super easy to create engaging and secure forms
- **Why it was picked**: Popularity and ease of use

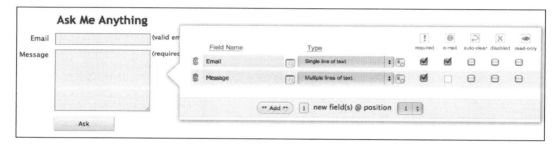

- **Manual Install URL**: `http://deliciousdays.com`
- **Automatic Install search term**: CFORMS
- **Geek level**: Webmaster
- **Configuration location: Top Navigation | cforms II**
- **Used in**: Posts, widgets, pages

WordPress lacks any methods for creating a form (beyond the comment form) to collect visitor questions, contact info, or any other type of communication data. CForms makes creating custom forms as easy as pointing and clicking. Forms can be embedded throughout your blog, including widgets, posts, and pages.

CForms administration

CForms is a very powerful and somewhat complex plugin, so let's take a moment to get familiar with the Administration section.

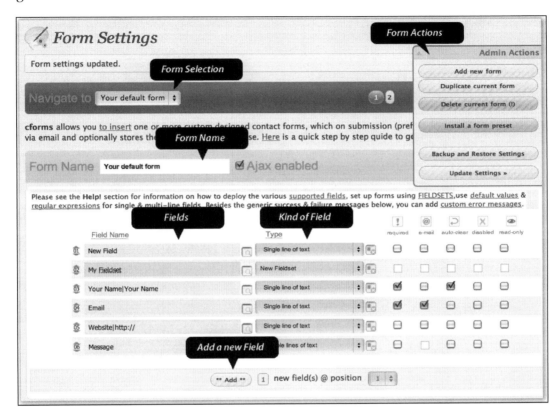

- Form Action is the somewhat hard-to-find **Admin Actions**. You will use this expandable menu to save your changes, delete, create, and back up your forms.

- Form Selection is how you switch between your different forms.

- Form Name is where you will define your form's name. This name will be used when you want to insert this form into a blog post, page, or widget.

- Fields are the individual inputs your form will contain.

- Kind of Field allows you to define a field as either a single line of text, multi-lined text, multiple-choice, captchas, file uploader, and a lot more.

- Add New Field will insert a new field into your form.

Modifying the default form

Once inside the CForms Administration, located at **Settings | CForms II**, you will see your "default form". This default form is the basic information needed to create a "Contact Us" form on your blog, including the field's name, e-mail, website, and message.

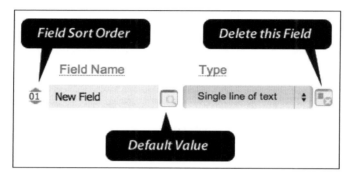

Click the **Field Sort Order** icon, and drag it to reorder the field to any other position. Use the **Default Value** icon to specify what the field's default value should be, as well as mouse over values and error messages. Use the **Delete this Field** icon to remove a field from your form.

Adding your form to a page, post, or widget

CForms can be inserted into pages, posts, and widgets. However, the widget version is awfully wide and will most likely not look right in your sidebar. At the time of writing, there is no apparent way to modify this.

Once inside the page or post editor, you will find a new icon added to your "Descriptions" toolbar.

Once you click the **CForms** icon, you will need to select which form you would like to include. The drop-down box will contain all of the forms you currently have active. If you would rather use the coding method to insert your form, use the WP tag `<!--cforms name="My Form Name"-->` or the PHP tag `<?php insert_cform("my form name"); ?>`.

Advanced CForms customizations

While CForms might not be the easier form/mailer plugin available, it is hands down the most flexible. Make sure to delve into the additional options towards the bottom of the *Form Manager*.

File upload settings

If you will be using the *File Upload* field, you will need to provide some additional server information for it to work properly. Specifically, you will need to define where your file should be uploaded to, the maximum file sizes, and what type of files are allowed to be uploaded.

Messages, text, and button label

Customize your buttons, error messages, and text non-fictions for a given form.

Core Form Admin / e-mail options

Inside the Core Form Admin, you will be able to turn on and off the ability to track submissions in the RSS feed, set redirection rules, set start and end dates when a form will be shown.

Admin e-mail message options

Configure the e-mail message that will be sent to the administrator, once a user submits a form—including setting which e-mail address to send to, the header and footer html, and the from e-mail address.

Auto confirmation

Automatically send your visitor a confirmation e-mail, once they submit a form by clicking the **Activate Auto confirmation** link. Through this option, you will be able to configure the subject and message to send, the moment a form is submitted.

Multi-part / multi-page forms

Create multiple page forms by activating the Multi-part form option. Once activated, the Multi-part forms panel will allow you to define what step the current form in your process is, along with the ability to add **back** and **next** buttons.

Tell-A-Friend form support

The *Tell-A-Friend* field must be activated before you can leverage it. Once activated, you will have a new field type called "tell-a-friend". This "field" is actually multiple fields that are required to tell a friend about a given web page.

WP comment feature

You can actually replace WordPress' comment system with CForms. This might be helpful if you would like to customize the fields that a user can submit on a comment, or if you want the user to be able to send the author an e-mail opposed to a public comment.

Third-party read-notification support

CForm offers integration with notification services `readnotify.com` and `didtheyreadit.com` to notify you if a user reads your e-mail. These services might cause your e-mails to be triggered as spam.

MapPress—Google maps

By Chris Richardson (`http://wphostreviews.com`)

- **Why it's awesome**: Easily hack together some neat mashups on Google's dime

- **Why it was picked**: Popularity, ease of setup

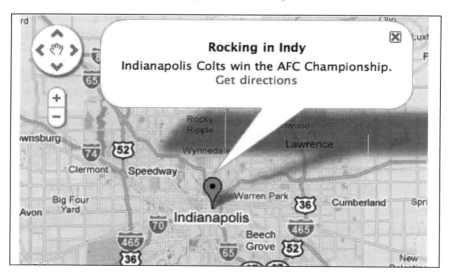

- **Manual Install URL**: `http://wordpress.org/extend/plugins/mappress-google-maps-for-wordpress/`
- **Automatic Install search term**: Mappress
- **Geek level**: Newbie
- **Configuration location**: **Settings | MapPress**
- **Used in**: Posts, pages

MapPress makes it easy to insert custom Google Maps into your blog. Once installed, you will have the option to add multiple locations by address or lat/long. You will need a Google Maps API-key, which can be obtained from `http://bit.ly/gmap-api`. Google requires users who customize maps to have an API key. This allows them to track usage and ensure that people are not using Google Maps outside the 'Terms and Conditions'. If you do not have a need for customizing the content on the map, then you could always bypass installing this plugin and use the embed code directly from Google Maps.

Adding a map to a post or page

You will now have a new panel titled MapPress during the editing or creation of a post/page. The MapPress panel is where you define the size of your map, and the specific points of interest.

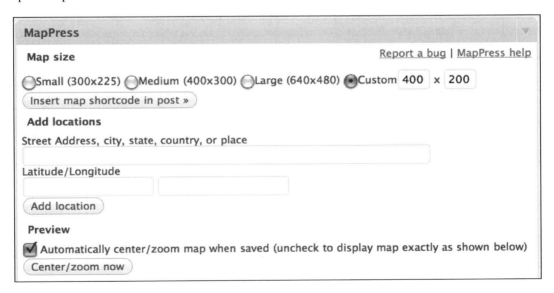

WP-O-Matic

By Guillermo Rauch (`http://devthought.com/`)

- **Why it's awesome**: Great for automatically pulling content from your other blogs or online applications
- **Why it was picked**: Flexibility and data import consistency
- **Manual Install URL**: `http://wordpress.org/extend/plugins/wp-o-matic/`
- **Automatic Install search term**: WP-O-Matic
- **Geek level**: WordPress Ninja
- **Configuration location: Settings | WP-O-Matic**
- **Used in**: Posts

WP-O-Matic is used to automatically create posts from an RSS or ATOM feed. This plugin is by far one of the more complicated plugins available, but insanely powerful. Imagine being able to take content from any website virtually, and automatically add it to your blog every time it is updated. With this plugin, you could hypothetically build a gigantic blog filled with tons of content, without ever manually posting.

Before you can begin, there are a few steps you need to go through to ensure that you have all of the right software available for this plugin to work. The first time you visit **Settings | WP-O-Matic**, you will be asked to click through a series of configuration options.

The first step makes sure that you have the right SimplePie installed. **SimplePie** is a wonderful piece of software that makes consuming RSS and ATOM feeds very easy.

The second step allows you to select how automatic updates will occur; your options are using a CRON job or a pseudo-automatic process. The **CRON** job does require you to do some server magic in the SHELL. For those of you who have no idea what that last sentence meant, uncheck the box at the end of the second step.

Creating your first campaign

In WP-O-Matic, a **campaign** is a collection of feeds (or a single feed) that will be imported into a specific area that you define. For example, let's say you want to create a new category dedicated to news about Space. Then you would create a new campaign called "Space news" that would contain multiple RSS feeds from other websites and blogs that write about Space. Then, on a schedule which you define, WP-O-Matic will automatically grab the latest news and create a post for each new item in the feed.

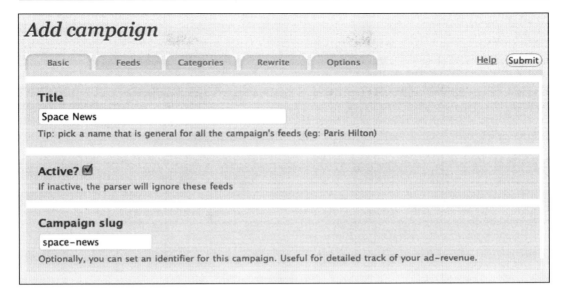

Adding feeds

The **Feeds** tab is where you will define each of the RSS or ATOM feeds you would like to include in your newly created campaign. WP-O-Matic has a great feature if you are unsure what the RSS feed is for a given website; all you have to do is provide the website's URL. For example, enter `http://universetoday.com`, and WP-O-Matic will automatically locate the websites' feed for you.

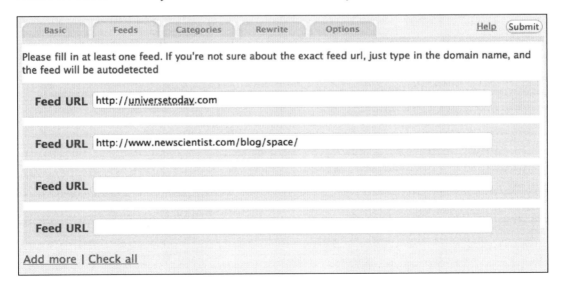

Categories

WP-O-Matic allows you to specify different categories for different feeds. This feature is awesome when you have a site that covers multiple topics and will be importing multiple types of content from different feeds.

Understanding WP-O-Matic's options

Each campaign has a slew of options available during import. The following is a breakdown of what each of the options will do.

- **Custom Post Template**: When WP-O-Matic is importing the text of a feed, you have the option of adding additional content to the post. This is helpful if you want to add a "Read More" link to the end of the post or include additional details about the feed.

- **Frequency**: By default, WP-O-Matic checks for new posts every day and a half. To change this to a different time delay, simply provide the number of days, hours, and minutes.

- **Cache Images**: Many times, feeds have images embedded in them. This setting automatically downloads the files to your own server. In this way, if the original publisher of the post deletes or changes an image, your blog still displays the original post images.

- **Perform Ping Back**: A **Ping Back** is a way to automatically notify another blog that you referenced one of their posts on your blog. If checked, the **Perform Ping Back** will automatically "ping" the blog post that WP-O-Matic adds to your blog. It's recommended that you check this option to give proper attribution for the posts you are importing.

- **Type of Post**: By default, new posts will automatically be published. You can change this setting by selecting either "draft" or "private".

- **Max items to create on each fetch**: Change the Max Items number if you want to import more than ten posts each time WP-O-Matic goes to work. Setting this number to 0 will import the maximum items in a feed.

- **Post title link to Source**: When a post is imported, you can either link the headline to the post on your blog or send the user directly to the original blog that posted the article.

- **Discussion Options**: Use the Discussion Options drop-down box to turn public commenting on or off.

Search unleashed

By John Godley (`http://urbangiraffe.com/`)

- **Why it's awesome**: Turns WordPress' basic search into a full text searching monster

- **Why it was picked**: Easy setup, multiple search algorithms

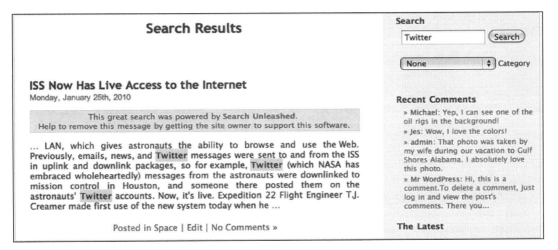

- **Manual Install URL**:
  `http://wordpress.org/extend/plugins/search-unleashed/`

- **Automatic Install search term**: Search Unleashed

- **Geek level**: Newbie

- **Configuration location**: Tools | Search Unleashed

- **Used in**: Posts, widgets, pages

Search is significantly more important than most people credit it. The ability to find content on your site is probably the most important aspect to running a successful blog. The Defacto search built in to WordPress is nice, but far from perfect. **Search Unleash** introduces powerful new methods to scour through your blog's data, including full text searching and Lucene powered searching.

Setting up your search index

A **search index** is a collection of information that is stored about each of your posts, pages, and other elements that contain text. This "Index" is then used during the searching process to quickly find the information that is relevant to the search terms provided by the user. Search Unleashed offers three types of search indexes.

 To select your search index type, click on "Options" within **Tools | Search Unleashed**

1. **Default WordPress**: The **Default WordPress search index** is what all WordPress blogs come with out of the box, and while this search is acceptable for most blogs, it's a bit slow and doesn't offer much intelligence.

2. **Full-Text Search**: As WordPress uses MySQL as its database, it's able to leverage MySQL's built-in full-text searching. MySQL's indexes are super fast, tested, and true. However, it can become slow when you are dealing with a blog that has more than 10,000 or more posts.

3. **Lucene**: **Lucene** is an open source product released by the Apache Foundation. The same company that brought us the insanely popular Apache web server that your blog most likely runs on. Lucene is the undisputed heavyweight in open source searching. With its unique searching and indexing algorithms, Lucene will absolutely deliver the search goods.

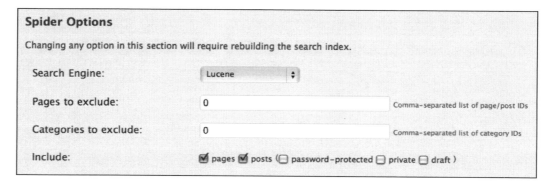

Creating your first index

Once you have decided on which Search Index to leverage, you will need to build your first Index; we highly recommend Lucene. If you have decided to use the default WordPress index, then you can skip this section.

 To run your first index, click **Search Index** from within **Tools | Search Unleashed**.

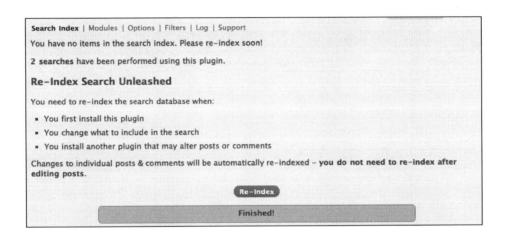

To initiate the indexing, you will need to click **Re-Index**.

Once you have completed your first index, you will not need to rerun it, as this process will now happen automatically. However, re-indexing your site is one potential solution if your blog search is not behaving properly, which can happen if data corruption happened during the indexing process.

WP Web Scrapper

By Akshay Raje (http://webdlabs.com/)

- **Manual Install URL**:
  http://wordpress.org/extend/plugins/wp-web-scrapper/
- **Automatic Install search term**: WP Web Scrapper
- **Geek level**: WordPress Ninja
- **Configuration location**: Settings | WP Web Scrapper
- **Used in**: Pages, posts

WP Web Scrapper is definitely not for the weak of heart, but it is for those of you who know what a "JQuery Selector" is. If you know what a "JQuery Selector" is, then you are in for one awesome coding treat. WP WebScrapper makes grabbing parts of ANY website and including it in a post or page on your blog, a snap!

WP Web Scrapper uses CURL and phpQuery to grab and manipulate data from any public website. Because WP Web Scrapper uses phpQuery, you have the luxury to select which elements you want from the external website using jQuery Selectors. Plus you do not need to be afraid if the external website changes, as WP Web Scrapper degrades gracefully if any changes occur.

Copyright warning

It's important to note that while WP Web Scrapper makes ripping content from a website super simple, it doesn't mean that it's legal. There are many big websites out there that will not take kindly to someone stealing their content. Make sure that you have permission before you take another website's content, or you might find a nice letter from some law firm in your mailbox.

Adding a scrapping

To create a new Web Scrapping, you edit a post or a page. Once installed, WP Web Scrapper will include a new button in your Toolbar that looks like a Gear.

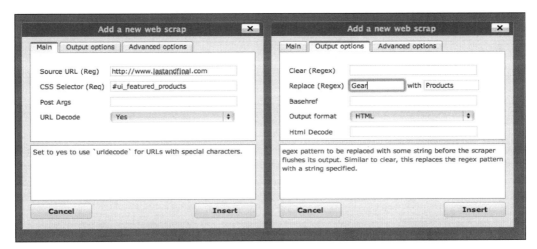

All that is needed for WP Web Scrapper to work is a valid website URL (**Source URL**) and a valid **CSS Selector**. Once you have added the external website's URL (don't forget the *http://*) and added your selector, click **Insert**. This plugin will create a short code that is inserted into the body of your post. Once you get familiar with the WP WebScrapper syntax, you will be able to add them without ever clicking the "Gear". For example:

```
[wpws url="" selector=".product" ]
```

Learn more about CSS Selectors by visiting
http://code.google.com/p/phpquery/wiki/Selectors

Summary

When it comes to blogging, content is king, both for your readers and for the search engine. The more unique content you spread on the internet, the better-off your blog will fare in this competitive landscape. In this chapter, we covered the following:

- GD Star Rating—add ratings and ranking to your blog content
- Better Tag Cloud—replace WordPress' default lackluster tag cloud with a customizable one
- Yet Another Related Posts Plugin—automatically link to similar posts throughout your blog
- My Page Order—easily reorder your blog's navigation with drag-and-drop ease
- Get Recent Comments—showcase the latest chatter on your blog
- Viper's Video Quicktags—quickly include videos from many popular sources
- WP Greet Box—greet your visitors differently, based on where they hail from
- NextGen Gallery—include dynamic and beautiful slideshows simply
- Zemanta—add context, images, and links to related content online
- CFormsII—build powerful forms
- MapPress—customizable Google Maps embedded into your blog
- WP-O-Matic—automatically pull and publish RSS and ATOM feeds
- Search Unleashed—give WordPress full text searching
- WP Web Scrapper—automatically pull content from your other websites

3
Sharing Content

Now that you have your blog loaded chock-full of juicy content, it's time to help your readers share it. Just one amazing post, the right reader, and the tools to re-tweet, post to Facebook, or share on StumbleUpon, can turn your blog into an overnight sensation.

In this chapter, we'll cover:

- How to let Twitter users share your blog posts
- How to let Facebook users share your blog posts
- Tracking downloadable content
- Using Google to host your blog's RSS feeds
- Creating and sending e-mail newsletters

TweetMeme

By Alex King (http://alexking.org/)

- **Why it's awesome**: Allows Twitter users to quickly share your blog post, and it tracks how often they do it
- **Why it was picked**: Super simple to install; no Twitter account is needed

- **Manual Install URL**: http://wordpress.org/extend/plugins/tweetmeme/
- **Automatic Install search term**: TweetMeme
- **Geek level**: Webmaster
- **Configuration location**: Top Navigation | TweetMeme
- **Used in**: Posts, pages

fuelinterface RT @use_this: Good designers want to be proved wrong, bad designers hope to be proved right http://bit.ly/bs6UM4 #ux
9:52 PM Feb 3rd from TweetMeme

The **TweetMeme** button is the fastest way to allow your readers to quickly share your blog posts to Twitter with a single click. In addition to offering this awesome sharing tool, you can also sign up for TweetMeme's analytic services to track the effectiveness of each of your posts.

Setting up TweetMeme

You can access TweetMeme's settings from the **Top Level Navigation** and then **TweetMeme | Settings**. The following is a list of the most important settings to focus on and what they do.

- **Display**: Choose this if you want to display the TweetMeme button on pages, on the home page, and within your feed
- **Position**: TweetMeme allows you to display the TweetMeme button in various positions around your blog posts—before, after, both before and after, shortcode, or manually
- **Type**: TweetMeme offers two types of buttons—normal and compact. By default, the normal button is displayed
- **Source**: Supply your Twitter username here, if you have one
- **URL Shortener**: Often, WordPress blog post URLs are rather lengthy and can eat up to many of the 140 characters Twitter allows. It recommends using Bit.ly for your URL shortening—Bit.ly has proven to be a resilient company that won't be disappearing any time soon.
- **TweetMeme API App ID & TweetMeme API App Key**: TweetMeme offers detailed analytics when people re-tweet your blog posts. This service is not free, but they do offer a free trial to get your hands dirty. To leverage TweetMeme analytics, you will need to create an account at http://my.tweetmeme.com, after which you will be able to find your API App ID and API App key from http://my.tweetmeme.com/profile.

Wordbook

By Robert Tsai (`http://www.tsaiberspace.net/`)

- **Why it's awesome**: You can share your posts to a user's Facebook wall

- **Why it was picked**: Ease of setup, integration level with Facebook

Brandon Corbin Totally Rad Geek Tattoos

Totally Rad Geek Tattoos
One must fully accept the fact that one is a nerd, and to be a nerd.
To be geeky without shame, and whenever possible publicly
profess one's love for the uncommon and the unquestioned. The
following tattoos are attached to such just individuals...

See More

February 2 at 11:11pm via Wordbook   Comment   Like   Read entire article

- **Manual Install URL**: `http://wordpress.org/extend/plugins/wordbook/`

- **Automatic Install search term**: Wordbook

- **Geek level**: Webmaster

- **Configuration location**: **Settings | Wordbook**

- **Used in**: Posts

Robert Tsai's **Wordbook** is an awesome way to get your blog posts listed on your Facebook profile or your Facebook pages. WordPress will post to Facebook a snippet of your post and a thumbnail of any images that might be in your post.

Once installed, you will see a red bar across your WordPress administrator section stating **Wordbook needs to be setup**—click the **Wordbook** link to start the configuration. In order to publish your posts to Facebook, you will need to connect your blog to Facebook—to start this process, click the blue Facebook button. Once you start the process, you will be redirected to Facebook to authorize WordPress to communicate with your Facebook account. Now, each time you create a blog post, WordPress will create a new shared item in your Facebook newsfeed.

WP Download Manager

By Lester Chan (http://lesterchan.net/)

- **Why it's awesome**: Quickly add downloadable files and media to your blog
- **Why it was picked**: Lester's plugins are legendary, they offer download tracking

---

💻 **FREE-Commerce Buttons** (397.7 KiB, 189 hits)

- **Manual Install URL**:
  http://wordpress.org/extend/plugins/nextgen-gallery/
- **Automatic Install search term**: WP Download Manager
- **Geek level**: Webmaster
- **Configuration location: Top Navigation | Downloads**
- **Used in**: Posts, pages

ID	File	Size	Hits	Permission	Category	Date/Time Added	Action	
1	FREE-Commerce Buttons » /ecommerce-buttons.zip *Last Updated: 9:51 pm, January 4, 2010* *Last Downloaded: 3:57 pm, February 6, 2010*	397.7 KiB	189	Everyone	Design	9:51 pm, January 4, 2010	Edit	Delete
3	LinkedIn Profile API » /linkedinProfile.zip *Last Updated: 2:43 pm, January 26, 2010* *Last Downloaded: 5:43 am, February 6, 2010*	10.5 KiB	271	Everyone	Software	2:43 pm, January 26, 2010	Edit	Delete
2	URL Summary » /urlsummary.zip *Last Updated: 10:05 am, January 25, 2010* *Last Downloaded: 4:04 am, February 6, 2010*	4.2 KiB	36	Everyone	General	10:05 am, January 25, 2010	Edit	Delete

It offers your readers the ability to download content. It is one sure fire way of increasing your blog traffic and the happiness of your readers. **WP Download Manager** makes managing and tracking downloaded files from your blog a snap.

Adding a new download

Start off by clicking **Add File** from the **Downloads** menu and follow these steps:

1. **File**: Select how you want to add a file:

    i. **Browse File** will show you a drop-down menu containing any files in the `wp-content/files` directory on your web server.

    ii. **Upload File** allows you to select any file from your computer to upload. The majority of the time, this is the method you will be using.

    iii. **Remote File** allows you to grab a file from any web server using a URL.

2. **File Name**: Give your download a human-readable name.

3. **File Description**: Supply a little information that will help your readers know what the file is about.

4. **File Category**: Select the category for this file. You can create new categories from the **Download | Download Options** menu.

5. **File Size**: Unless you are using the Remote File method, leave this field blank. WP Download Manager offers automatic detection of file size, but sometimes it will not work properly on Remote Files.

6. **File Date**: If you need to back-date your file, you can use this field to do so. However, the majority of the time you will leave this field alone.

7. **Starting File Hits**: If you want to make your download look more popular, you can pad the number of downloads.

8. **Allowed to Download**: If you want to limit downloads only to readers who are subscribed and logged in, use this drop-down menu to control who can download. Your options are **Everyone, Registered Users Only, Contributors, Authors, Editors**, or **Administrators**.

9. Click **Add File**.

Inserting a download into a post

Now that we have a new file uploaded to the Download Manager, we need to make it accessible to our readers. The WP Download plugin will add a new button to your WYSIWYG menu on posts and pages.

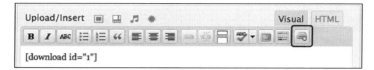

One downside to WP Download is that you have to know the ID of the file you want to include in your post or page. Once you click the Download button, provide the **download id** in the pop-up window. You can find the ID of your file by clicking **Download | Manage Downloads**; the first column will contain the ID of the download.

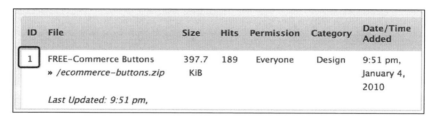

ID	File	Size	Hits	Permission	Category	Date/Time Added
1	FREE–Commerce Buttons » /ecommerce-buttons.zip	397.7 KiB	189	Everyone	Design	9:51 pm, January 4, 2010
	Last Updated: 9:51 pm,					

Twiogle Twitter Commenter

By Twiogle (http://twiogle.com/)

- **Why it's awesome**: Quickly fills your blog's comments with somewhat relevant content
- **Why it was picked**: Easy to set up, works exactly as advertised

- **Manual Install URL**: http://wordpress.org/extend/plugins/twiogle-search/
- **Automatic Install search term**: Twiogle Commenter
- **Geek level**: Newbie
- **Configuration location**: Settings | Twiogle Twitter Commenter
- **Used in**: Posts, pages, widgets

Twiogle Twitter Commenter has a horrible name, but an awesome result. If your blog is lacking in comments and chatter, this plugin will automatically add new ones from recent tweets. It works its magic by taking the tags from your blog post and searches Twitter for tweets that use the same tags. To really take advantage of this plugin, you need to make sure you add tags to your blog posts; the more specific your tags are, the more relevant the comments that will be imported.

With any service that automatically adds content to your blog, you need to keep an eye on it. It is very much possible for your comments to get overrun with pointless Twitter chatter if you run this plugin for too long.

ShareThis

By Sharethis (http://sharethis.com)

- **Why it's awesome**: Gives visitors the ability to share your blog posts using virtually every type of service they might already use
- **Why it was picked**: Dead simple to install, longevity of the product

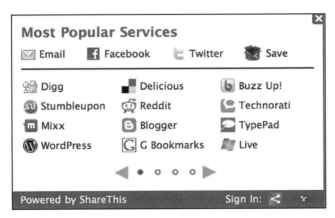

- **Manual Install URL**: `http://wordpress.org/extend/plugins/share-this`
- **Automatic Install search term**: Sharethis
- **Geek level**: Newbie
- **Configuration location**: Settings | ShareThis
- **Used in**: Posts, pages

ShareThis is one of the most popular sharing widgets available online today. While this service is not specifically built for WordPress, it does offer a plugin for easily adding this sharing service to your blog.

Setting up ShareThis

To get ShareThis working properly on your blog, you will first need to register a free account with ShareThis at `http://sharethis.com/publishers/register`.

Once you have created an account, copy the code from the **Your Code** textbox.

Home / Publishers / **Get the Code**

Step 3: Install

- Download the plugin archive, and expand it.
- Put the 'ShareThis' folder into your 'wp-content/plugins' directory (end up with: 'wp-content/plugins/share-this/<files>').
- Go to your WordPress Administration area and navigate to the Plugins page then click "Activate" the ShareThis plugin.
- Go back to your WordPress Administration area:
  - For Wordpress 2.6 and earlier, navigate to the Options page then click the ShareThis tab.
  - For Wordpress 2.7, click on Settings on the left side to open the menu, and click on the ShareThs link in the Setting Menu
- Copy and paste the javascript code in the box provided, and click the update button.

Your Code:

```
<script type="text/javascript"
src="http://w.sharethis.com/button/sharethis.js#publisher=6973d532-d428-4ca6-80f5-
9ddf4f23dea7&amp;type=wordpress&amp;style=rotate"></script>
```

Once you have copied the ShareThis code, you will need to paste it into the ShareThis code within the ShareThis plugin.

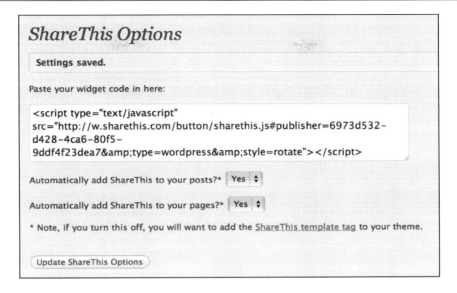

Wibiya Bar - Beta

By Wibiya (http://wibiya.com/)

- **Why it's awesome**: Add tons of functionality to your blog using a toolbar at the bottom of the users screen

- **Why it was picked**: Easy to setup, lots of plugins and customizations available

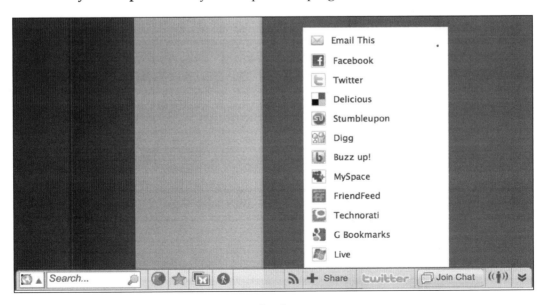

- **Manual Install URL**: http://wibiya.com
- **Automatic Install search term**: Not Available
- **Geek level**: Webmaster
- **Configuration location**: **Appearance | Wibiya Configuration**
- **Used in**: Site-wide

Wibiya is a free service that allows you to include a toolbar at the bottom of your website or blog. Even though Wibiya is still in the beta stage, this killer toolbar can be customized to include a slew of applications that can make your blog truly unique. By default, the Wibiya bar includes a site-search that is powered by Google, a site-wide chat room powered by TinyChat.com, live webstats, a sharing button for pushing to all of your social media sites, and much more.

Unlike the other plugins discussed in this book, Wibiya is not specific to WordPress. In fact, Wibiya can be included in any website. However, the team at Wibiya did make a tiny WordPress plugin that makes getting the bar on your WordPress blog very easy.

Installing the Wibiya bar

1. Visit http://wibiya.com, and click **Get it Now**.

2. Create an account.

3. Pick the color for your bar.

4. Pick the apps for your bar.

    Note that some of the apps require usernames; if you do not want to promote your Facebook or Twitter profiles, you will need to deselect these applications by simply clicking on the apps icon:

    i.   Supply your social media usernames.

    ii. Select the WordPress icon (the big W in a circle).

    iii. Download, install, and activate the plugin.

Caution

Try to control the urge to install every application they offer. The more apps you add, the slower your website will load. Each of these applications are JavaScript-based and can quickly add significantly more code than what needs to be loaded by each visitor.

WP Facebook Connect

By Adam Hupp (http://hupp.org/adam/)

- **Why it's awesome**: Makes integrating your blog with WordPress super easy
- **Why it was picked**: Depth of integration, no coding required

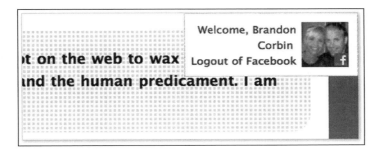

- **Manual Install URL**: http://wordpress.org/extend/plugins/wp-facebookconnect
- **Automatic Install search term**: WP FacebookConnect
- **Geek level**: WP-Ninja
- **Configuration location**: **Settings | Facebook Connect**
- **Used in**: Posts, pages, widgets, comments

WP Facebook does require a little coding within your blog's theme. However, the coding is minimal and will help expose you to very basic PHP, if you are not already familiar with it.

Creating an app ID for your blog

Facebook Connect requires you to set up a Facebook application to communicate between Facebook and your blog.

1. Visit http://www.facebook.com/developers/createapp.php.
2. For the sake of organization, give your application the name of your blog or something similar.

3. Facebook will automatically generate an **API Key** and **Secret**—each of these keys will be required to complete the setup of the WP-FacebookConnect plugin.

4. In the **Settings | Facebook Connect**, provide your **API Key** and **Secret**.
5. Click **Update Options**.

Once you have set up your plugin, your website will automatically include a Facebook badge in the upper-right-hand corner of your website. If a user is logged into Facebook, they will see their name and their avatar.

Adding the connect button to your comments

In most cases, a user will want to connect their Facebook account to leave a comment on your website. To have a 'connect to Facebook' button on your comments page, you will need to edit your themes in the comments.php file.

Locate the `comments.php` in **Appearance | Themes | Editor**. Select the `comments.` `php` and insert the following code to add the **Facebook Connect** button at the end of the file:

```
<?php do_action('fbc_display_login_button'); ?>
```

Twitter Friendly Links

By Konstantin Kovshenin (`http://kovshenin.com/`)

- **Why it's awesome**: Creates very short URLs for you blog
- **Why it was picked**: Easy to install, nice widget

- **Manual Install URL**: `http://wordpress.org/extend/plugins/twitter-friendly-links/`
- **Automatic Install search term**: Twitter Friendly Links
- **Geek level**: Webmaster
- **Configuration location**: **Settings | Twitter Friendly Links**
- **Used in**: Posts, pages

Thanks to Twitter's 140 character limit, an entirely new marketplace bubbled up—insanely short URLs. Companies like `Bit.ly`, `TinyUrl.com`, and `is.gd` offer to shrink your huge URLs in return for super tiny ones.

One problem with these types of URL shrinkers is that you ultimately lose control of your URLs. If any of those services went out of business, so would all of those links you plastered over Twitter, Facebook, and LinkedIn.

Twitter Friendly Links helps you regain that control over your links in a very simple and brilliant way—by transforming your long URL like `http://domain.` `com/2010/10/my-blog-post-title` to `http://domain.com/a1234`.

Feedburner Feedsmith

By Steve Smith & Feedburner (`http://feedburner.com/`)

- **Why it's awesome**: Never having to worry about nefarious uses of your RSS feeds

- **Why it was picked**: Built by the Google crew at Feedburner

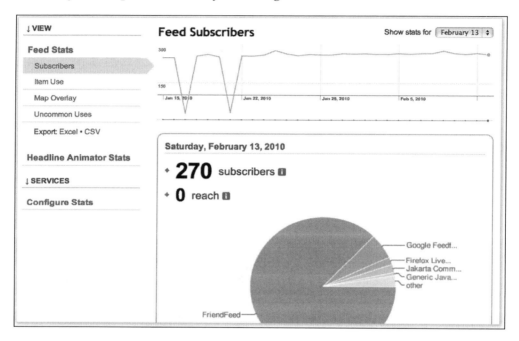

- **Manual Install URL**: `http://www.google.com/support/feedburner/bin/answer.py?hl=en&answer=78483`

- **Automatic Install search term**: Not available

- **Geek level**: Webmaster

- **Configuration location: Settings | Feedburner**

- **Used in**: Feeds

Many times, hosting your own RSS feed can wreak havoc on your server without you ever knowing it. Due to RSS's out-of-sight-out-of-mind style, you often forget about it completely. Using Google's **Feedburner** is one way to ensure that a swarm of subscribers won't bring your server to a crawl. Feedburner acts like a conduit to your RSS feed by delivering the feeds from Google's servers instead of your own.

Not only does Feedburner offload your server traffic, it also gives you an amazing view of what people are doing with your feed. The stats alone are worth signing up.

Burning your feed

Submitting your feed to Google will take only a few minutes, but the rewards are long lasting.

Create a Google account

You will need to have a Google account to leverage Feedburner. If you do not already have an account with Google, you can sign up at `https://www.google.com/accounts/NewAccount`.

Verify your blog's feed URL

Each WordPress blog comes with RSS feeds enabled. To access your feed, go to `http://yourdomain.com/feed/`.

Burn your feed

Now we must set up a new feed to burn by visiting `http://feedburner.google.com` and adding our feed to the **Burn a feed right this instant** input box.

Name your feed

Once you have added your feed, you will need to name the feed and create a URL to use it. Your feed title should be something descriptive about your blog, as this is what all of your RSS subscribers will see as the title of your blog.

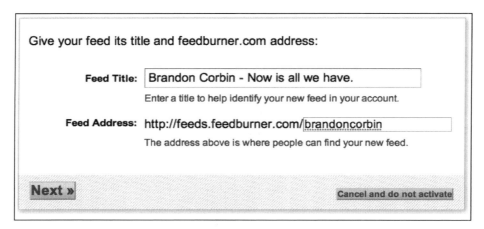

Configuring WP-Feedburner

Now that you have your feed hosted on Google, we can finish the process of setting up WP-Feedburner. WP-Feedburner's configuration is located in **Settings | WP Feedburner**.

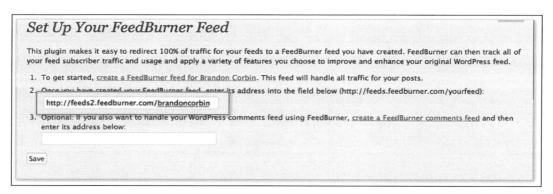

Your feed should now be officially set up to redirect to your Feedburner feed. To make sure everything is working properly, visit `http://yourdomain.com/feed/` and check that the URL gets redirected automatically to the Feedburner URL that you set up earlier.

SendIt

By Giuseppe Surace (http://www.giuseppesurace.com/)

- **Why it's awesome**: Send e-mail campaigns for free
- **Why it was picked**: Easy to set up and free

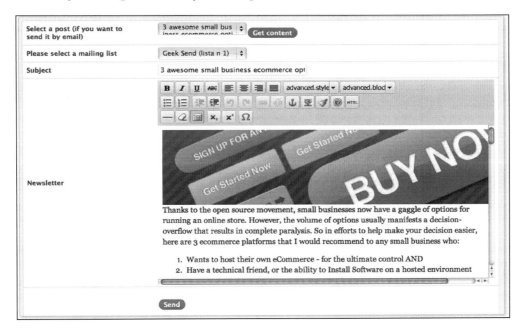

WARNING: This plugin is still in the beta stage, but the majority of the functionality works great.

- **Manual Install URL**: http://wordpress.org/extend/plugins/sendit/
- **Automatic Install search term**: SendIt
- **Geek level**: WP Ninja
- **Configuration location**: **Top Navigation | Newsletter**
- **Used in**: Newsletters

SendIt has more potential to change the way you communicate with your readers than any other plugin mentioned in this book. SendIt was originally written in Italian, and every once in a while, you will stumble on to a few words that are yet to be translated. However, besides the occasional Italian noun, SendIt is very straightforward and makes running multiple newsletters as easy as managing your blog.

SendIt overview

Unlike other plugins, SendIt is a fairly large plugin with multiple configuration pages and areas to set up, tweak, and perfect.

- **Newsletter**: Compose and send your newsletters from the Newsletter section
- **Manage subscribers**: Add and remove e-mail addresses from a given newsletter
- **SMTP settings**: If you are planning on using SendIt to send to more than 600 subscribers, you might want to consider setting up an external SMTP server for sending your mail. Otherwise, you can leave this section alone
- **Newsletter settings**: Find, delete, and edit newsletters
- **Import emails from comments**: Quickly build e-mail lists from everyone who has commented on different blog posts
- **Import emails from WP Users**: Quickly build e-mail lists from other writers, users, and administrators on your blog

Creating your first newsletter

For the purpose of this example, we will create a Geek Newsletter for our blog readers to subscribe to.

1. Start by visiting **Newsletter | Newsletter Settings**.
2. Click **Create New List**.
3. A new list will automatically be added to your **Available Lists** grid.
4. Select **Edit** from the newly created list.
5. Define the **From** e-mail address, newsletter name, and the header and footer for this newsletter template. The header and footer will automatically be applied for each e-mail you send from this mailing list.
6. Click **Save**.

Adding subscribers

A mailing list is only as valuable as the readers who follow them. SendIt offers a few different ways to add subscribers to your newsletters.

Automatic import

SendIt allows you to automatically import the e-mail address of everyone who has commented on your blog or has signed up for your blog. These one-click importers can be found at **Newsletter | Import Emails from Comments** and **Newsletter | Import Emails** from WP Users.

Auto importing e-mail addresses might not be CAN-SPAM compliant. It's suggested to only use the Subscription Widget and fight the temptation to auto-subscribe these people. You can learn more about the CAN-SPAM laws at `http://www.ftc.gov/bcp/edu/pubs/business/ecommerce/bus61.shtm`.

SendIt Widget

Along with the cool newsletter features, SendIt has a widget to let users subscribe quickly to a given newsletter. You will find the SendIt Widget in **Appearance | Widgets**.

You will need to know the **Mailing List ID** for this widget for it to function properly. To locate the Mailing List ID, visit **Newsletter | Newsletter Settings**.

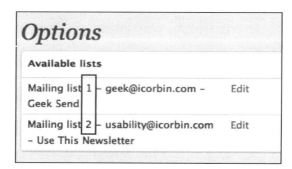

It's important to remember that this software is still in the beta stage. There are obvious parts that are still missing. However, I have no doubt the next version Giuseppe releases will meet virtually all of those requirements.

Specifically, you currently do not have a way to edit the title of the widget. However, you can customize the look and feel if you know CSS, as Guiseppe did a wonderful job labeling his markup.

Sending a mail

Sending a newsletter is very similar to writing a blog post using the same WYSIWYG editor. Additionally, you can load a newsletter's content from any existing blog post. To start writing a newsletter campaign, click on the **Newsletter | Newsletter** link in your navigation.

- **Select a Post**: This field is optional, even though it's the first input field and feels deceptively important. However, if you want to send your mailing list something quickly, there's nothing better than pulling from something you have already written.

- **Please Select Mailing List**: This drop-down box contains each of the mailing lists you have created. Each time, you will need to select which mailing list to send a particular mail to.

- **Subject**: The subject of a newsletter should be something catchy, short, and obvious.

READ BEFORE SENDING:
As of Version 1.4.6, when you click **Send**, it sends—for real, no preview nor pre-warning, it just starts sending. We can accept that these features will be added later on, but just be aware that when you send, IT SENDS!

Subscribe-Remind

By Trevor Fitzgerald (`http://trevorfitzgerald.com/`)

- **Why it's awesome**: Helps increase readership
- **Why it was picked**: No configuration, promotes subscriptions

If you enjoyed this post, make sure you subscribe to my RSS feed!

- **Manual Install URL**:
  `http://wordpress.org/extend/plugins/subscribe-remind/`
- **Automatic Install search term**: Subscribe-Remind
- **Geek level**: Newbie
- **Configuration location**: No Configuration
- **Used in**: Posts

RSS subscribers are wonderful customers; they continually allow us to feed our content directly into their desktop, mobile phone, and maybe even their website. Why not try to get as many of them to sign up as possible? **Subscribe-Remind** is a gentle plugin that gives the reader the opportunity to subscribe to your RSS feed.

This plugin is perfect for those new to blogging and WordPress. However, if you are looking for more choices and features, our next plugin is just what you're looking for.

Once installed, your readers will be presented with a little dialog box towards the top of your blog inviting readers to **Subscribe to my RSS feed!**.

Sociable

By Blogplay (`http://blogplay.com/`)

- **Manual Install URL**: `http://wordpress.org/extend/plugins/sociable/`
- **Automatic Install search term**: Sociable
- **Geek level**: Webmaster
- **Configuration location**: **Settings | Sociable**
- **Used in**: Posts

Sociable, like many other social bookmarking plugins, gives your readers the ability to share, post, or e-mail your webpage to a handful of sources.

Sociable is different in so many options they provide, both in social media outlets and plugins configuration. Also, Sociable is lightweight both in file-size and render–time, as compared to some of the fancier looking Share Me tools.

Visit the settings page at **Settings | Sociable** to enable which sites you want to present on your blog as a sharing option. You are also able to drag-and-drop to reorder the list to your hearts content. If you're looking for beauty, then go with the *Sexy Bookmarks* section mentioned in *Chapter 2, Generating Content*; otherwise Sociable is a great, fast, and passably attractive solution.

Understanding social options

Part of Sociable's appeal is its customizability; its options are aplenty, giving you control that other plugins can only dream about. To start customizing Sociable, visit **Settings | Sociable**.

Disabling sprite usage for images

A **sprite** is a single image that contains every possible icon Sociable offers; if you are only showing one or two services, it is recommended to avoid the 45KB file size of the sprite and just go with the individual images.

Disabling alpha mask on the share toolbar

By default, the icons are shown at 50 percent opacity and this turns to 100 percent once the user rolls over the service icon. This option allows you to turn this feature on and off.

Tagline

Customize the little message that incentivizes your readers to share your wonderful blog post. By default, the message is **Share and Enjoy**.

Position

By default, the Sociable toolbar appears under each of your blog posts. Sociable gives you the option to place the toolbar on:

1. Front page of the blog.
2. Individual blog posts.
3. Individual pages.
4. In category archives.
5. Tag listings.
6. Date-based archives.
7. Author archives.
8. Search results.
9. RSS feed items.

Use Text Links

If you would rather just display the text of the service's name instead of the icon, make sure this option is checked.

Image Directory

Sociable is awesome for designers who blog, in that they give you the ability to replace the default icons with your own icons. This is done by simply changing the image directory path to a new one that contains your own icons.

Use Thisbox/iFrame on links

This option will create a lightbox effect with an embed iframe on your webpage, instead of sending the reader to a new webpage.

Open in New Window

Another way to keep readers on the site is to open these links in a new window, instead of the current window the reader is on.

Awe.sm

Sociable can automatically shrink your URLs to fit within the often-limited space provided by tools like Twitter and Facebook. You will need an `Awe.sm` account that can be obtained from: `http://awe.sm`.

Summary

Sharing is a human trait; why should our websites and blogs be any different? With the previous plugins mentioned, your content and ideas can now be easily spread through the blogosphere.

- TweetMeme—Readers can RT your blog post on twitter
- Wordbook—Sharing your post on Facebook
- WP Download Manager—Track, control, and limit file downloads
- Twiogle Twitter Commenter—Automatic comments from twitter posts
- ShareThis—Service to share your blog post to many social networks
- Wibiya Bar—Cool website tool bar with lots of great apps
- WP FacebookContent—Connecting Facebook and your blog
- Twitter Friendly URLs—Give your blog tiny URLs without the use of a third party
- Feedburner Feedsmith—Offload your RSS delivery to Google
- SendIt—Create targeted e-mail newsletters
- Subscribe Remind—Give your readers a little reminder to subscribe to your RSS feed
- Sociable—Highly customizable social sharing

The next chapter's plugins will help you create a super functional and beautiful blog, including automatically creating a mobile version of your site.

4
Style and Function

In this chapter, we will focus on making your blog accessible, functional, and beautiful. Today, more than ever, users are accessing websites from billions of different devices ranging from browsers, smart phones, dumb phones, netbooks, and even televisions. In order to keep up with this rapidly changing environment and to keep readers engaged, your site has to adapt to the users as opposed to the user having to adapt to your blog. With the following plugins installed, your blog will become user-focused and stand out from the crowd of 10 million other blogs.

In this chapter, we will cover:

- Making your blog mobile
- Sending notifications to your mobile phone
- Letting users pick their theme
- Adding design details to your blog
- Inserting dynamic content into posts and pages

About Me Widget

By Sam Devol and John BouAntoun
(`http://samdevol.com/` & `http://jbablog.com`)

- **Why it's awesome**: Great to talk shamelessly about yourself
- **Why it was picked**: Simple setup

- **License**: GNU General Public License
- **Manual Install URL**:
  `http://wordpress.org/extend/plugins/about-me-widget/`
- **Automatic Install search term**: About Me Widget
- **Geek level**: Newbie
- **Configuration location**: **Appearance | Widgets**
- **Used in**: Widgets

This simple widget allows you to toot your own horn from your blog's sidebar. The **About Me Widget** gives you a full blown WYSIWYG (what-you-see-is-what-you-get) editor within the widget's configuration panel.

Setting up your About Me Widget

Once you have installed the About Me Widget, visit **Appearance | Widgets** and locate the **About Me Widget** listed in the **Available Widgets** panel. Click and drag the widget to one of your sidebars. Expand the widget's configuration panel and start shamelessly promoting yourself!

Category Posts Widget

By James Lao (http://jameslao.com/)

- **Why it's awesome**: Target posts by category from your sidebar
- **Why it was picked**: Easy to use, increased search engine optimization benefits

- **License**: GNU General Public License
- **Manual Install URL**: http://wordpress.org/extend/plugins/category-posts/
- **Automatic Install search term**: Category Posts
- **Geek level**: Newbie
- **Configuration location**: **Appearance | Widgets**
- **Used in**: Widgets

Want to promote a specific set of posts? **Category Posts Widget** allows you to list out recent blog posts on your sidebar by category. To add the widget, visit **Appearance | Widgets** and drag the **Category Posts Widget** to your sidebar.

Depending on the theme you are using, you will need to try out the different configurations and see how they look overall. In many themes we tested, displaying the **Post Excerpt**, **Post Date**, and **Number of Comments** results varied on how well the end result looked. However, most themes should display things properly when you only display the headline of each post.

After the Deadline

By Automattic (http://blog.afterthedeadline.com/)

- **Why it's awesome**: Beyond grammar checking, makes you a better writer
- **Why it was picked**: Simple installation, configurability, how well it works

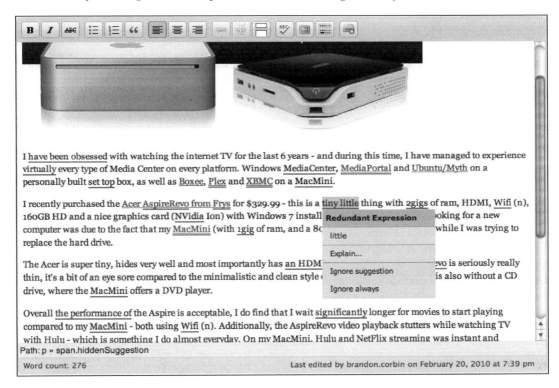

- **License**: GNU General Public License
- **Manual Install URL**:
  http://wordpress.org/extend/plugins/after-the-deadline/
- **Automatic Install search term**: After the Deadline
- **Geek level**: Newbie
- **Configuration location**: Users | Profile
- **Used in**: Posts, pages

After the Deadline fills a massive void that exists in WordPress, which is the ability to really proofread your content. This plugin, created by the company that owns Wordpress.com, is an indispensible resource to help ensure that your content is written with proper grammar. On top of spell checking and basic grammar checking, After the Deadline digs deeper into your content looking for all sorts of writing no-nos.

Using After the Deadline

After the Deadline is available in the post and page content editor. Once you have written your post or page, simply click the icon with the ABC and a checkmark.

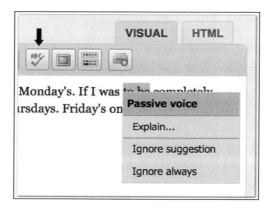

Once you click the plugin icon, After the Deadline will start analyzing your content for common grammatical errors and less common mistakes, often made by writers, including: passive voice, double negatives, bias language, clichés, jargon, and much more. Errors will become underlined and clickable. Once clicked, a menu will expand, showing you the mistake and offer suggestions on how to correct it.

WordPress Mobile Pack

By James Pearce

- **Why it's awesome**: Works great, even on non-smart phones
- **Why it was picked**: Skins both the blog and the administration, browser support

- **License**: GNU General Public License

- **Manual Install URL**: http://wordpress.org/extend/plugins/wordpress-mobile-pack/

- **Automatic Install search term**: WordPress Mobile Pack

- **Geek level**: Webmaster

- **Configuration location: Appearance | Mobile Theme, Mobile Widgets, Mobile Switcher**

- **Used in**: Everything!

There are 6.5 billion people on Earth; 1.5 billion of them have cell phones. More and more of those 1.5 billion cell phones are browsing the web. Some of them are smart phones with awesome browsers, but the majority of them use the older and far less sexy WAP (wireless access protocol) versions of websites. Designing a blog to work on the iPhone, Blackberry, Android, Palm's WebOS, and every other cell phone variation would be insanely time consuming, unless you use **WordPress Mobile Pack**.

Not only does WordPress Mobile Pack make your blog easy for your readers to follow on their mobile phone, it also converts your entire WordPress administration into a nomad admin's wildest fantasy. Edit, create, and delete posts, approve and reply to comments, and even switch your theme, all from the palm of your hand.

Mobile themes

Once you have installed WordPress Mobile Pack, you will now have **Appearance | Switcher** in your navigation. Use the **Theme Switcher** to select which mobile theme you want to use for any user visiting your blog from a mobile phone. The theme you select will not affect any normal computer or web browser users.

Browser detection and domain detection

WordPress Mobile Pack offers two methods for determining if a user is using a browser on a mobile device, browser detection, and domain detection.

Browser detection will leverage the information your browser sends to a website that identifies what type of device is requesting the web page and which browser it's using.

Domain detection allows you to use a subdomain like m.yourwebsite.com to display the mobile version of our blog.

 Domain detection does require some server setup, including setting up Apache to send the subdomain requests to point to your WordPress installation. Thus browser detection is recommended for our less technical readers.

Important Mobile Themes settings

The majority of setup options for WordPress Mobile Pack are located in **Appearance | Mobile Theme**.

- **Enable Nokia Templates**: Nokia is still the heavyweight in mobile devices, the biggest selling point of this plugin over WP-iPhone, which focuses purely on Webkit-based browsers on Android, Palm Pre, iPhone, and now Blackberry. If you aren't worried about Nokia users, then we would recommend using WPTouch that's covered in the next section.

- **Check Mobile Status**: By clicking on **Launch ready.mobi**, you'll be taken to Ready.mobi's service for validating. Now, your website is ready for mobile devices.

- **Number of Posts**: By default, WordPress Mobile Pack will only show five posts per page. However, remember that the more posts you show, the longer your website will take to load on these bandwidth-constrained devices.

- **Teaser Length**: A teaser is a sneak peek of content from an entire blog post. By default, WordPress Mobile Pack will display 50 characters from the beginning of your blog posts.

- **Remove Media**: A lot of mobile devices don't handle Flash, movies, or embedded frames very well. By default, WordPress Pack will remove these media references from the mobile version of your blog. It's recommended that you uncheck this option as more and more devices can now handle videos from sites such as YouTube.

- **Shrink Images**: WordPress Mobile Pack offers the option to automatically shrink larger images to help reduce the overall download of your website. If you are having problems with file permissions and don't know how to change server folder permissions, you might want to uncheck this option.

- **Simplify Styling**: In another step to ensure that your blog looks great across multiple devices, WordPress Mobile Pack will automatically remove custom stylings from your blog posts. More advanced users should most likely uncheck this option.

WPTouch

By BraveNewCode (http://www.bravenewcode.com/)

- **Why it's awesome**: Incredibly cool mobile version of your site for modern day smart phones

- **Why it was picked**: Look and feel, configurations, icons—it's just beautiful!

- **License**: GNU General Public License
- **Manual Install URL**: `http://wordpress.org/extend/plugins/wptouch/`
- **Automatic Install search term**: WPTouch
- **Geek level**: Webmaster
- **Configuration location**: **Settings | WPTouch**
- **Used in**: Pages, posts, comments

For readers who find WordPress Mobile Pack's user experience lacking and are less concerned with a blog that can be browsed in any Nokia device, they will rejoice with WPTouch. **WPTouch** is an insanely well designed and thought-out plugin that turns your blog into one powerful mobile WebApp.

WPTouch not only offers an excellent user experience for Android, iPhone, Palm Pre, and some BlackBerry devices, it also has built-in support for a bunch of popular WordPress plugins for Caching, Tweeting, and more.

The previous screenshot shows WPTouch's beautifully laid out navigation.

Web App icon

WPTouch's default icon is shown on the top-level navigation bar, when a mobile user bookmarks your website to their home screen. WPTouch offers a slew of predesigned icons for everything from music to movies and every Web2.0 service out there.

Page icons

In the WPTouch's settings menu, you can define which pages to show and which icon to display next to that page.

Creating your own icon

If you're not crazy about the default icons, which are mainly used for page icons, they give you a very easy way to upload your own image that will be converted into the iPhone/iPod Touch's home screen icon. For the icons to look correct, images should be 32 x 32 pixels and either a PNG, JPG, or GIF image type. If you're not sure how to make your image meet these specifications, WPTouch offers a quick link to FlavorStudios' iPhone Icon Generator: http://www.flavorstudios.com/iphone-icon-generator.

Push notifications

If you're running an iPhone or Android application, make sure to check out WPTouch's Prowl integration. Prowl lets you get instant notifications when users take specific actions on your website, like commenting, for example.

WP-Prowl

By Nathan Wittstock (http://milkandtang.com/)

- **Why it's awesome**: Push notifications to your iPhone when specific events happen on your blog
- **Why it was picked**: Real time notifications, configurability

- **License**: GNU General Public License
- **Manual Install URL**: http://wordpress.org/extend/plugins/wp-prowl/
- **Automatic Install search term**: WP-Prowl
- **Geek level**: Webmaster
- **Configuration location**: **Settings | WP-Prowl**
- **Used in**: Comments, new user registration, direct messages

To understand what **Prowl** is, you first need to understand what Growl is. **Growl** is a small application that runs on your Mac or PC that other applications can leverage to create non-obtrusive notifications on your computer. For example, if you're running the Instant Messenger client Adium and a friend sends you a message, Growl will display a small message in the upper-right-hand corner with a snippet of the message, giving you the option to either respond or ignore.

Growl is an open source project that can be downloaded for free. Download Growl for the Mac from http://growl.info/ or for the PC from http://www.growlforwindows.com. While Growl is not required for this plugin, it's a great free utility that's well worth installing.

Prowl is basically Growl for the iPhone/iPod Touch. At the time of writing this, it's not available for any other device. So if you don't have an iPhone or iPod Touch, it's safe to skip this plugin entirely.

Now that we got rid of those non-iPhone users, you are in for a treat. Prowl makes keeping up with the actions on your blog instantaneous. Each time a reader leaves a comment you get a notification. If a new user registers at your blog, guess what—another notification.

Setting up WP-Prowl

Setting up Prowl requires an account on the Prowl website and an API key to let WP-Prowl validate your account.

1. Visit the Prowl website `http://prowl.weks.net/` and register for a free account.
2. Once you have registered, click the **Settings** tab and copy your **API key**.
3. Go back to your blog's admin and visit **Settings | WP-Prowl** and paste your **API key** in to the input box.
4. Purchase ($2.99) and download the Prowl iPhone app from Apple's AppStore: `http://bit.ly/prowlapp`.

Now that you have WP-Prowl configured, you will get a push notification on your iPhone or iPod Touch each time someone leaves a comment, talks about one of your posts on another blog, or creates a new post.

Favicons

By Loane (`http://www.webonews.fr/`)

-   **Why it's awesome**: A handful of nice default icons to spruce up your blog's address bar
-   **Why it was picked**: Available icons, design quality, and ability to upload your own designs

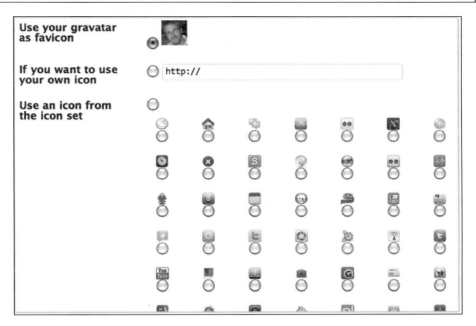

- **License**: GNU General Public License
- **Manual Install URL**: http://wordpress.org/extend/plugins/favicons/
- **Automatic Install search term**: Favicons
- **Geek level**: Newbie
- **Configuration location**: **Settings | Favicons**
- **Used in**: Entire site

A **Favicon** is that little icon that is displayed next to your browser's address bar in the browser's tab or Windows toolbar. Additionally, search engines often display a website's favicon next to its search results.

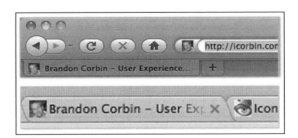

Most people who are running a smaller site rarely pay attention to the Favicon. At face value, this tiny image doesn't seem important, but in fact, the favicon has more brand power than any other graphic on your website. Because the favicon is displayed on every single page, I would go as far to say that the favicon is even more important than the site's main logo. Unfortunately, to get a favicon running, you have to know the `<meta>` tag details and how to create an ICO image file. Luckily, the Favicon plugin makes it a no brainer.

Setting up your Favicon

If you have a Gravatar account (`http://gravatar.com`), the Favicons plugin will display your main Gravatar image as your favicon. If no Gravatar image exists, then you will need to decide if you want to use an icon from the Favicon gallery or use an image from any image URL. To get started, visit **Settings | Favicons**.

Picking from the gallery

The Favicons plugin offers over 100 free Favicons to pick from, covering a slew of things like Twitter to Smiley, Faces to Poker Cards. To use a pre-designed icon, select **Use an icon from the icon set**, and then select the radio button below the icon you would like to use.

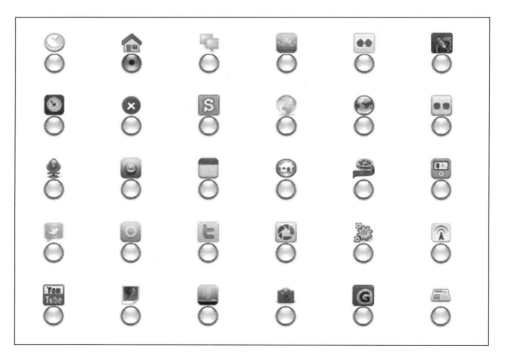

Use your Gravatar as Favicon

Select **Use your gravatar as favicon** to automatically have your Gravatar icon used as your Favicon. Gravatar is a great service that allows you to manage your avatar or profile image for multiple websites from one place. WordPress, by default, supports Gravatars for comments, and each day more and more sites are adding Gravatar support. You can sign up for a free Gravatar account at `http://gravatar.com`.

Using a remote icon

Select **If you want to use your own icon** and enter the URL to any `.png` or `.ico` file online. By default, Favicons display at 16 by 16 pixels. While larger images can be used, it might not look quite right. Of course, you should obey all copyright laws, but websites like `http://iconfinder.net` and others allow you to search through lakhs of free icons.

Theme Switcher

By Ryan Boren (`http://ryan.boren.me/`)

- **Why it's awesome**: Users can customize your blog to their style
- **Why it was picked**: Dead simple installation, giving visitors a custom experience

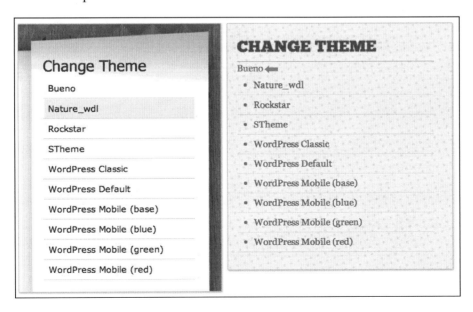

- **License**: GNU General Public License
- **Manual Install URL**: `http://wordpress.org/extend/plugins/theme-switcher/`
- **Automatic Install search term**: Theme Switcher
- **Geek level**: Newbie
- **Configuration location: Appearance | Widgets**
- **Used in**: Widgets, site-wide

Theme Switcher allows your readers to select available themes from your sites. Once selected, each time the visitor returns, they will be treated to the custom theme they picked.

Once installed, you will have a new **Theme Switcher Widget** to select from **Appearance | Widgets**. This widget allows you to display the available themes either as a **List** or a **Drop-down Menu**.

Advanced marketing use

If you're a company that markets to multiple channels/markets, Theme Switcher could easily be transformed into a **Select Your Market**, where each market/channel is a custom theme that is designed and written specifically for its demographic. For example, if you market to home buyers and renters, you could create two different themes with unique home pages, one called **For Home Buyers** and another called **For Renters**. When a home buyer clicks **For Home Buyers**, the site will change to the **For Home Buyer** theme, and from then on, the user will experience the **Home Buyer** version of your blog/website.

Image Widget

By Shane and Peter, Inc (`http://www.shaneandpeter.com/`)

- **Why it's awesome**: Easily add images to your blog's sidebar without any HTML
- **Why it was picked**: Works exactly as advertised

Product of the Week

Listy.me, sharable lists.

- **License**: GNU General Public License
- **Manual Install URL**:
  `http://wordpress.org/extend/plugins/image-widget/`
- **Automatic Install search term**: Image Widget
- **Geek level**: Newbie
- **Configuration location**: **Appearance | Widgets**
- **Used in**: Widgets

Sometimes, all you want is a single image in your blog's sidebar, and that's exactly what Shane and Peter built. The **Image Widget** allows you to easily upload and select an image to display with a link, description, and title.

Post Layout

By Satollo (http://www.satollo.net/)

- **Why it's awesome**: Quickly insert HTML in to multiple parts of a post
- **Why it was picked**: Flexibility, Satollo's reputation as a plugin developer, configurability

- **License**: GNU General Public License
- **Manual Install URL**:
  http://wordpress.org/extend/plugins/post-layout/
- **Automatic Install search term**: Post Layout
- **Geek level**: Webmaster
- **Configuration location**: **Settings | Post Layout**
- **Used in**: Posts, pages

Post Layout is a remarkable plugin that allows you to dynamically inject HTML before, after, and in the middle of posts and pages. Before, if you wanted to insert Google Adwords or put a link at the bottom of every post, you'd need to edit your themes source files directly. While this is possible, the next time you switch themes your customizations will be gone and you will need to edit the newly selected theme. Post Layout solves this problem by storing the customizations in the database and inserts the content dynamically, regardless of the current theme.

In addition to inserting content in posts and pages, Post Layout also lets you specify different content for mobile users. To enable mobile detection, you will need to select **Enable Mobile user agent detection** in **Settings | Post Layout**.

Inserting content

To help get you started, let's try to add a follow me on twitter link to the bottom of each of your posts.

First, you will need to visit **Settings | Post Layout**. To create the link, we will need to modify and insert the following code, replacing [YOUR-TWITTER-USERNAME] with your actual Twitter username:

```
<div style="text-align:center;
   margin:5px;
   padding:5px;
   border-bottom:solid 1px #CCCCCC;">
   <a href="http://twitter.com/[YOUR-TWITTER-USERNAME]">
     Do you follow me on twitter?
   </a>
</div>
```

Insert the code into the **Before the content** textarea, and click **Save**, located at the bottom of the page.

Now when your visitors read your blog post, they will be able to quickly click through to your Twitter account. In addition to any HTML tag, you can use the following short tags in each of the textareas, which will be dynamically replaced with the content from the post the visitor is currently reading.

- [title] will be replaced with the post or page's full title
- [title_encoded] will be replaced with a URL-safe version of the post or page's title
- [link] will be replaced with the post or page's full URL
- [link_encoded] will be replaced with a URL-friendly (encoded) version of the post or page's full URL
- [author_aim] will be replaced with the author's AOL Instant Messenger name

Breadcrumb NavXT

By Mtekk and Hakre (`http://mtekk.weblogs.us/`)

- **Why it's awesome**: Adds a navigation trail of your visitors' current position on your blog

- **Why it was picked**: Clean code for styling, easy setup, and installation

- **License**: GNU General Public License
- **Manual Install URL**: `http://wordpress.org/extend/plugins/breadcrumb-navxt/`
- **Automatic Install search term**: Breadcrumb Navxt
- **Geek level**: Webmaster
- **Configuration location**: **Settings | Breadcrumb NavXT**
- **Used in**: Home, posts, pages

Breadcrumbs are a very common feature to help users identify where they are in a website. For some reason, WordPress out of the box doesn't have any built-in methods for dynamically creating this common design pattern. Fortunately, Mtekk and Hakre decided to take matters into their own hands and created **Breadcrumb NavXT**. This plugin creates a new PHP function to include in your posts and pages templates that generate a dynamic Breadcrumb.

You will find a slew of configuration options that allow you to control how your blog's breadcrumbs will render. However, you might also notice that even once you installed the plugin, your blog still doesn't have a breadcrumb! Don't fret, this plugin requires you to add some code manually to your theme's template files.

Inserting the Breadcrumb

The reason this plugin got the geek rating of Webmaster is specifically due to the fact that to leverage this plugin, you must edit your theme. Luckily, the process is fairly painless.

1. Visit **Appearance | Editor** and select either **Single Post** or **Page Template** from the list of available theme files.

2. Locate the top of your post's content within the page's HTML. This area is often located right above the code `<?php while (have_posts() : the_post(); $count++; ?>`.

3. Insert the Basic Breadcrumb snippet of code at the top of the page.

Basic Breadcrumb

```
<div class="breadcrumb">
<?php
  if(function_exists('bcn_display'))
  {
    bcn_display();
  }
?>
</div>
```

Exec-PHP

By Soren Weber (`http://bluesome.net/`)

- **Why it's awesome**: Execute PHP code directly in posts
- **Why it was picked**: Pure power, ultimate customizability

- **License**: GNU General Public License
- **Manual Install URL**: http://wordpress.org/extend/plugins/exec-php/
- **Automatic Install search term**: Exec-PHP
- **Geek level**: WP Ninja
- **Configuration location**: **Settings | Exec-PHP**
- **Used in**: Posts, pages, text widgets

 Exec-PHP should not be used by most common bloggers because it gives too much power to the user. Be warned that running this plugin can be a huge security threat, and should be used only under adult supervision.

Exec-PHP's ability to execute PHP directly into a post, page, or text widget is one of the simpler yet more powerful plugin features available. However, like Peter Parker's uncle said, "With great power comes great responsibility". Exec-PHP should be installed with care and respect.

With this plugin enabled, your website runs a higher security risk, simply because PHP code, which is stored in the database, is executed on the server. If your database is compromised, a hacker can easily execute server-side PHP scripts without ever needing to access the server files.

Security concerns aside, once Exec-PHP is installed, you will be able to put any PHP code directly into a post, page, or text widget, and it will be executed when a visitor hits that resource.

Using Exec-PHP to list your latest tweets

In this example, we will pull in an RSS feed from Twitter and display the results in a page called My Tweets.

1. Create a new page by clicking **Pages | Add New**.
2. Tile the page as My Tweets.
3. Click the **HTML** tab.
4. Insert the following code snippet.

```
<?
$feedurl = "http://twitter.com/statuses/user_timeline/55928594.
rss";
$feed = simplexml_load_file($feedurl);
?>
div class="twitter-container">
  <? foreach($feed->channel->item as $tweet) { ?>
```

```
      <div style="font-weight:bold; padding:3px;">
      <? echo $tweet->description; ?>
      <a href="<? echo $tweet->link; ?>">Read Tweet</a>
      </div>
   <? } ?>
</div>
```

5. Click **Preview**.

Your page should now contain a list of posts from @use_this, including the tweet and a link to view the tweet on Twitter. Hypothetically, any RSS feed can be inserted into the $feedurl variable. However, this snippet will not work well for ATOM-based feeds.

To find your Twitter RSS feed, visit your Twitter profile page http://twitter.com/brandoncorbin, right-click on the **RSS feed of username's tweet**, and select **Copy URL**. Replace the $feedurl variable with the URL to your Tweet's RSS feed.

Summary

Focusing on the design and user experience of your blog not only helps your readers, but also shows that you care about them.

- WordPress Mobile Pack—Instantly turn your blog into a mobile platform

- WPTouch—Make your blog beautiful on the iPhone, iPod Touch, and Android

- WP-Prowl—Send notifications directly to your iPhone/iPod Touch

- After the Deadline—Ensure your posts are grammatically correct

- Favicons—Quickly create a favicon for your website

- Theme Switcher—Give your readers the ability to pick a theme

- Post Layout—Inject code before, after, and in the middle of posts and pages

- Exec-PHP—PHP code execution in posts and pages

- Image Widget—Easily insert an image into your sidebar

- About Me Widget—Promote your awesomeness from your sidebar

- Category Post Widget—Display the latest posts from a given category

- Breadcrumb NavXT—Display a breadcrumb for a user's current location in your blog

In the next chapter, you will learn how to turn your blog into a mini-social network using the BuddyPress plugin.

5
Building a Community with BuddyPress

Unlike our previous chapters, building a community will revolve around a single killer plugin—**BuddyPress**. The crew at Automattic, the company that owns Wordpress.com, released BuddyPress in April of 2009 in order to add basic social networking features to WordPress. Since then, BuddyPress has continued to be updated and tweaked and is now, hands down, the best community-building plugin available for WordPress.

In this chapter, you will learn:

- The basics of starting an online community
- What BuddyPress does
- How to install BuddyPress
- Setting up BuddyPress
- Leveraging other social networks to drive traffic
- BuddyPress plugins to customize your community

Before setting up BuddyPress

The most important step to building a community is defining your "Community Purpose". While this seems like an obvious statement, more often than not, people who start an online community fail to pick their niche or fail to stick to it.

You shouldn't just start an online community about anything and everything, mainly because the market is already dominated with these types of sites; unless you are completely mad or backed by billions of dollars—taking on Facebook or Twitter wouldn't be recommended.

Picking your market and determining what the purpose of your community will be, will make the process of creating your community significantly easier, finding community members easier and will help search engines know exactly what your website is about.

Simply stating that you want to have the biggest network with X users is not a valid Community Purpose. Instead you want to be as detailed as you possibly can within 140 characters; something like "Building a community that will connect extreme sport enthusiasts to share ideas, tips, and products". Once defined, write down your Community Purpose and put it wherever you can see it on a daily basis.

Sticking to your Community Purpose

It's very tempting to want to change your focus when you see your initial traffic is less than stellar; fight this urge with every ounce of your being. It takes time to build a sustainable community. No matter what your traffic numbers are, keep adding focused content to your site and eventually Google will start sending traffic your way.

BuddyPress

By Andy Peatling and John James Jocoby (http://buddypress.org/developers)

- **Why it's awesome**: Instant Social Network, just add water
- **Why it was picked**: Tons of features, easy installation

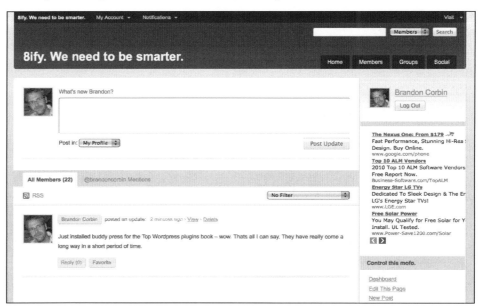

- **License**: GNU General Public License
- **Manual Install URL**:
  `http://wordpress.org/extend/plugins/buddypress/`
- **Automatic Install search term**: Buddypress
- **Geek Level**: Webmaster
- **Configuration Location**: **Top Navigation | BuddyPress**
- **Used in**: Most things

BuddyPress features

BuddyPress is a social network in a single plugin. BuddyPress's features will instantly transform your standard WordPress site into a wonderful social network that, on a feature-to-feature comparison, will compete with other networks like `Ning.com`, Facebook, and even Twitter. The following items pinpoint some of the great features that your blog will now possess. Additionally, you can visit `http://buddypress.org/demo/` to see all of the features live.

Smooth member signup

One of BuddyPress's features that make it killer is the super simple account creation process. No longer are users presented with the default WordPress Registration page. Instead, they see a nicely designed and simple form for picking a username, supplying their e-mail, and a password.

Create an Account

Registering for this site is easy, just fill in the fields below and we'll get a new account set up for you in no time.

Account Details

Username (required)

brandon

Email Address (required)

null@icorbin.com

Choose a Password (required)

••••••

Confirm Password (required)

••••••

Profile Details

Name (required)

brandon

Complete Sign Up →

Twitter-like posting

Each user of your BuddyPress community will be able to post short messages to their profile page or to any group they are a member of. Unlike Twitter, there is no 140 character text limit on the posts.

In addition to Twitter Style posts, BuddyPress offers threaded discussions. A threaded discussion is a conversation that allows you to reply inline to the previous message. Twitter on the other hand offers no threaded discussions and opted for a single thread that requires a user to create a new post with the @username reply method.

Profiles

Just like Facebook and Ning, BuddyPress offers a customizable Profile page for your community users.

Member communication

BuddyPress allows community members to send each other personal and private messages. Each time a private message is sent, the receiver is notified via e-mail and is driven back to your website—a great viral feature!

Forums

Online forums have been around longer than actual web pages. Known as **BBS (Bulletin Board Systems)** back in the day, they still play a massive role in engaging community members to return to your site.

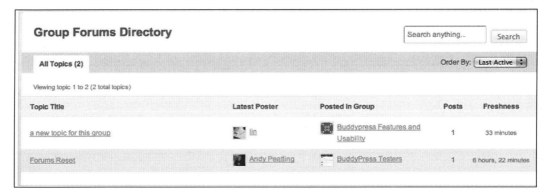

Groups

Groups are a way to segment your audience and offer a free exchange of ideas. This metaphor exists on virtually every type of social network, except Twitter. Groups are a great way to help your community members meet others with similar interests.

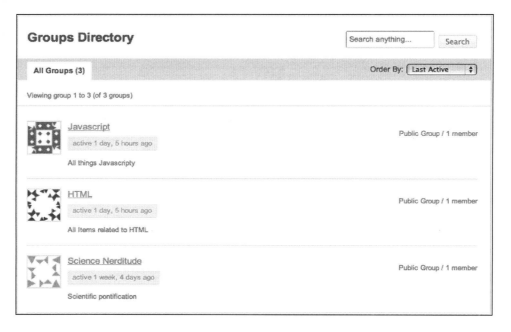

Members Directory

What's a social network without a **Members Directory**? BuddyPress's **Members Directory** allows other members to search and filter other members as well as request them to be "friends". BuddyPress took the same approach which Facebook took regarding "befriending" other members, as both parties need to approve the connection. This is unlike Twitter's method where anyone can follow another user without their permission.

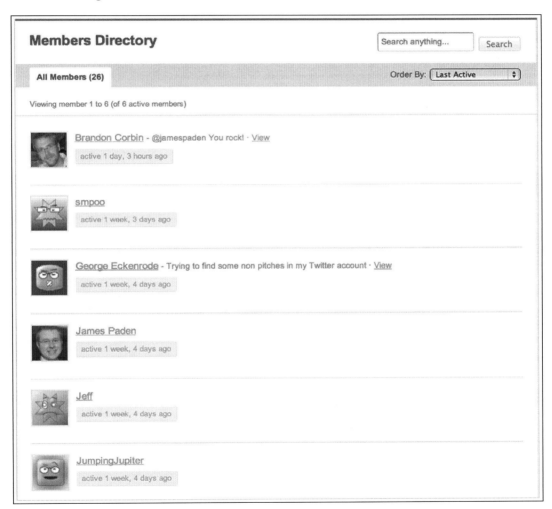

BuddyPress themes

As BuddyPress includes many options, most of the free WordPress themes will not suit your needs. Unless you are prepared to completely customize a traditional WordPress theme, it's recommended that you pick one that already supports all of BuddyPress's features. By default, BuddyPress includes a blue-tabbed theme which should suit the needs of most users. However, if you need something different, here are a few other BuddyPress supported themes.

Cosmic Buddy

You can visit the following URL to find out about **Cosmic Buddy**:

```
http://buddydev.com/buddypress/cosmic-buddy-the-free-theme-to-turn-
your-buddypres-to-orkut-style-site/
```

BP Nicey

You can visit the following URL to find out about **BP Nicey**:

```
http://buddydev.com/buddypress/bp-nicey-a-simple-and-clean-child-
theme-for-buddypress/
```

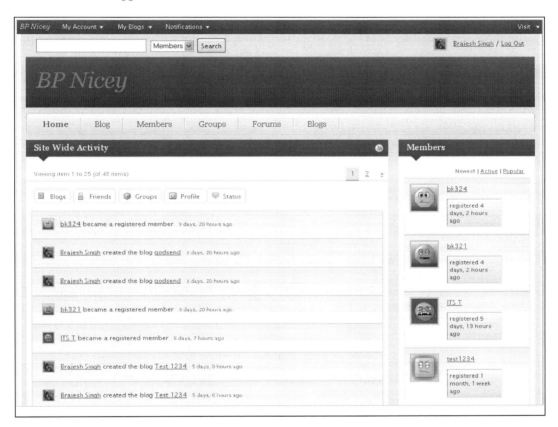

Sense and Sensibility BP 1.6

You can visit the following URL to find out about Sense and Sensibility:

`http://freebpthemes.com/onsite/sense-sensibility/`

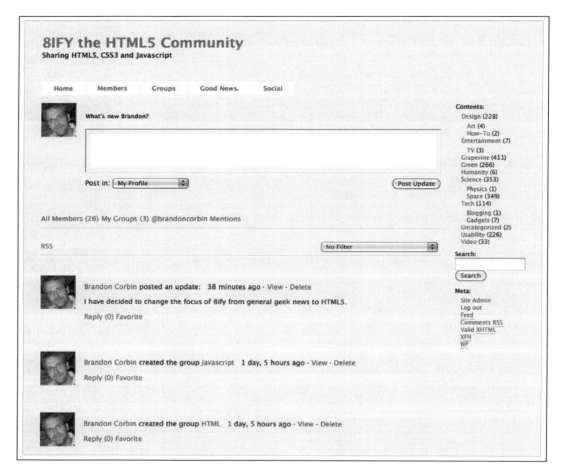

More themes

Unfortunately, there are very few BuddyPress themes, compared to the hordes of standard WordPress themes available. As the popularity of BuddyPress rises, the numbers of available and free themes should follow. Like WordPress, BuddyPress has its own library of available themes at `http://buddypress.org/extend/themes`.

BuddyPress plugins

Virtually all WordPress plugins will work with a BuddyPress WordPress site. However, the reverse is not always true. BuddyPress plugins will require you to have BuddyPress installed.

The following items are a few plugins which are available to customize your community that much more. Unfortunately, at this time, the number of plugins available specifically for BuddyPress is about as thin as the number of themes available for BuddyPress.

To find more BuddyPress-specific plugins, visit http://buddypress.org/extend/plugins.

Group Documents

By Peter Anselmo and Studio66 (http://www.studio66design.com/)

- **License**: GNU General Public License
- **Manual Install URL**: http://wordpress.org/extend/plugins/buddypress/
- **Automatic Install search term**: Buddypress Group Documents
- **Geek Level**: Webmaster
- **Configuration Location: BuddyPress | Group Documents**
- **Used in**: Groups

The **Group Documents** plugin creates a new page within each of your groups that allows users to upload any type of file or document. These documents can be edited or deleted by the individual who originally uploaded the document, the group administrator, or the site administrator. This plugin also gives you two new widgets to show the most recent documents uploaded and the most popular.

TweetStream

By Peter Hofman (`http://www.faboo.nl/`)

> **TweetStream is an awesome plugin to connect BuddyPress and Twitter http://bit.ly/bgk0fH**
> about 2 hours ago via 8ifyConnect

- **License**: GNU General Public License
- **Manual Install URL**: `http://wordpress.org/extend/plugins/tweetstream/`
- **Automatic Install search term**: TweetStream
- **Geek level**: Webmaster
- **Configuration location**: **Top Navigation | TweetStream**
- **Used in**: Profile, home, status updates

TweetStream is a very easy-to-set-up plugin that allows your members to connect their accounts to their Twitter account. Once installed, every time a member pushes a status update, he/she has the option to post it to their Twitter profile. Optionally, users can automatically sync their profile status between their site and Twitter. If the user chooses this option, each time when they tweet on Twitter, it will automatically be posted to their profile page on your BuddyPress site.

Connecting to Twitter

Start by clicking **TweetStream** in your WordPress administrator's top navigation. The first section focuses on the Twitter API credentials—specifically looking for your **Applications Consumer Key** and **Consumer Secret Key**.

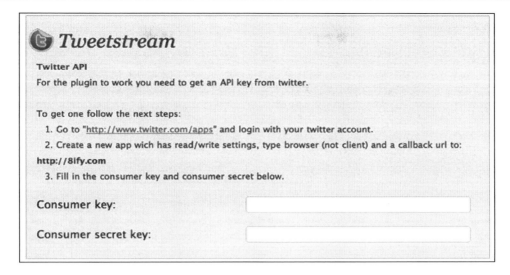

To find the **Consumer Key** and **Consumer Secret Key**, you will need to create an application on Twitter.

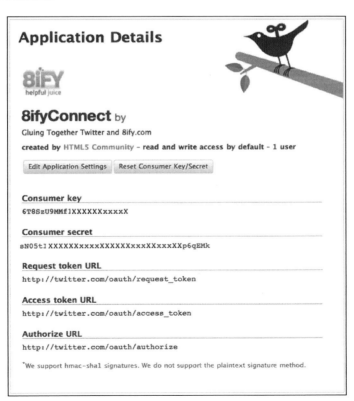

- Visit `http://twitter.com/apps`; if you're not already logged into the right Twitter Account, you will be prompted to log in
- Click **create an application**
- Copy the consumer key and paste it into the **Consumer key** input field of TweetStream
- Copy consumer secret key and paste it into the **Consumer secret key** input field TweetStream

Once you have connected Twitter and your BuddyPress site, each member who has not yet connected their Profile to their own Twitter account will see the following message: **Want to tweet this message to? Check your tweetstream settings**.

BuddyPress Album+

By Francesco Laffi and foxly (`http://flweb.it/`)

- **License**: GNU General Public License
- **Manual Install URL**: `http://wordpress.org/extend/plugins/bp-album`

- **Automatic Install search term**: BuddyPress Album+
- **Geek level**: Newbie
- **Configuration location**: **BuddyPress | BP Album+**
- **Used in**: Profile, albums

Much like Facebook, **BuddyPress Album+** adds complete photo album management for each of your community members. Users can upload pictures to their albums along with adding titles, descriptions, and custom privacy options. The privacy options include public, visible to members, visible to friends, and private. Additionally, your members will be able to turn commenting on or off, on a photo level.

As the administrator, you can globally enable or disable comments on photos and control how thumbnails are displayed in your user stream.

Setting up your Community Groups

Groups are an instrumental key to segmenting your social network. A group is simply an area that you create to help facilitate communication between each member. Like LinkedIn Groups, members of your community will request to become a member of the group. Once a member, users can post directly from their status update to any of the groups to which they belong.

Step 1: Group details

- Group Name: The name of the group; this field is required.
- Group Description: A short paragraph about the group; this field is also required.

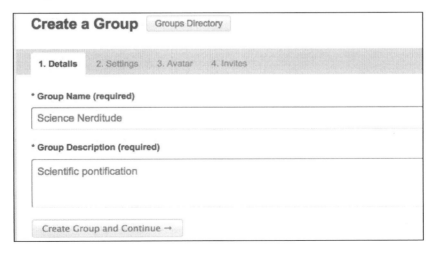

Step 2: Settings

Each group can have different privacy settings. The settings tab allows you to configure which type of privacy this group should respect.

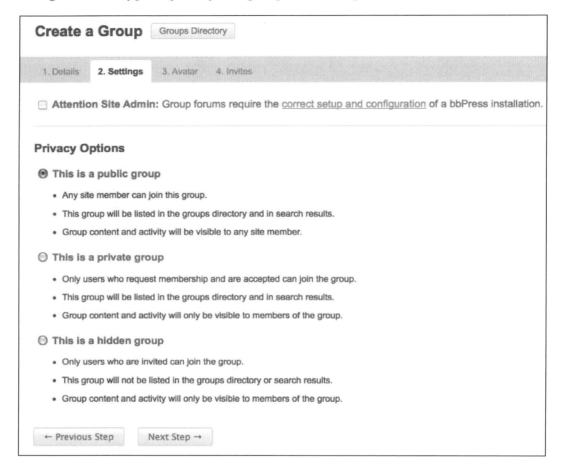

Step 3: Avatar

Avatar is the little icon that represents what the group is about. By default, BuddyPress has a handful of generic icons that will be randomly picked if you do not provide an avatar.

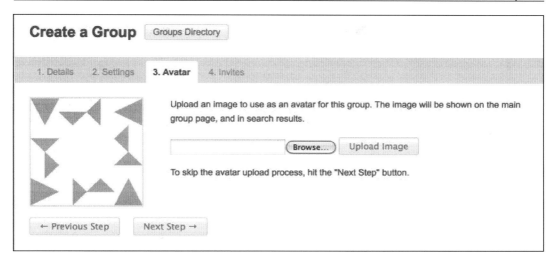

Tips for driving traffic to your community

A community without people isn't much of a community. There are many methods to help drive traffic to your website initially; here are a few tips and suggestions.

Friends and family

Once your website is ready to launch you'll need someone to pass on the word. The most popular websites ever—including Facebook, Twitter, HotOrNot, and countless others—got their first blast of traffic by sending out a single e-mail to all of their friends announcing their new website, and asking for their friends to tell others. In the case of Facebook, this single e-mail sent by Mark Zuckerberg turned into an incredible viral loop which is still going six years later. Create a compelling e-mail explaining your Community Purpose and send it to as many friends and family members as you can muster.

Social networks

Twitter and Facebook have become virtually a must-have resource for any website that's starting up. With a collective reach of over a billion users and with all of the tools available to make posting to them a snap, there is absolutely no excuse for not using them.

Twitter

You absolutely must have a Twitter account—hopefully one that has the same name as your domain name, minus the domain extension. For example, com, .net, .me.

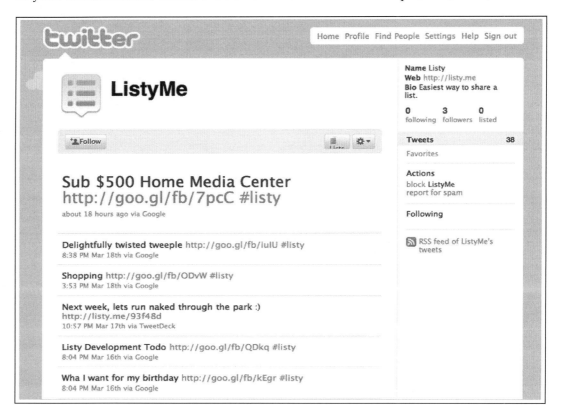

Once you have created your Twitter account, make sure to install the Twitter Tools plugin, mentioned in *Chapter 1, Plugin Basics*. Ensure that each of your blog posts are automatically pushed to your new Twitter account and that your Twitter profile contains a link back to your website. Once you have a handful of Tweets, begin the process of following individuals who meet your Community Purpose. WeFollow, http://wefollow.com, is a great website to help find the top Twitter users for any given topic. Start off by following at least 100 people; hopefully this will lead to 20 percent following you back and even a higher percentage visiting your website.

Facebook

Regardless of whether you like Facebook or not, this social juggernaut is simply too large to ignore. To get going on Facebook, you will need to create an account for yourself, if you do not already have one. Do not set up an account for your website like it's a person, as Facebook specifically disallows this activity. Instead, you will need to create a "Fan Page" off your personal Facebook profile.

A Facebook fan page is much like a unique person on Facebook, with the obvious difference that other members become **Fans** opposed to **Friends**. To create a Facebook page, visit http://www.facebook.com/pages/create.php.

Once your **Fans** page is created, you should use an RSS application like RSS Graffit, http://www.facebook.com/RSS.Graffit, to have each of your new blog posts automatically posted to your Fan Page.

Google AdWords

Google AdWords' allows you to create and run advertisements for your website insanely quickly. Your ad will be run on both Google's website and their advertising network that consists of millions of other websites.

Sponsored Links

Usability Experts
We specialize in **usability** & design
of portals and complex applications
www.TandemSEVEN.com

Improving **Usability**
Great web sites focus on **usability**
We will guide you to greatness!
www.**usability**sciences.com

HTML5 Community
Get your HTML5, CSS3
and Javascript on!
www.8ify.com

See your ad here »

Your ads will be displayed along the search results when someone searches Google using one of your keywords. These are the ads under the **Sponsored Links** located in the right side of the search page. Google offers a variety of different ad formats including: text ads, image ads, and video ad units.

Thanks to Google AdWords ability to limit the total spent on a daily basis, you could be running a campaign today regardless of your budget. You also get to pick the total amount you are willing to pay for a click. Keep in mind that the lower your Cost Per Click, the lower down the sponsors list your ad will display.

Create a Google Adwords account and start marketing at
`http://google.com/adwords`.

Google search

After six months of your site being live, Google will most likely be the largest source of traffic to your website (that is, of course, unless you are using some unsavory search engine optimization tactics). The following is a very high-level view of how the Google Bot works.

Google has an amazing ability to find your new site through countless avenues. The most obvious method is seeing your website talked about by other websites that Google sees as being important and relevant. You can also tell Google about your new website by submitting it to the Google Webmaster Tools (`https://www.google.com/webmasters/tools/home?hl=en`)

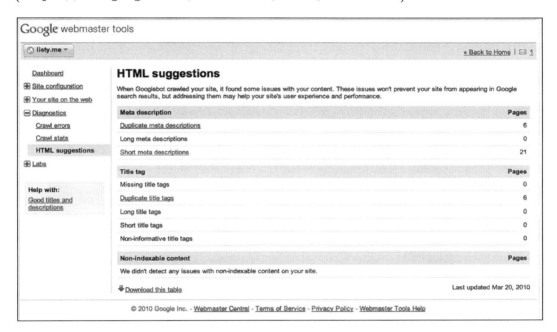

The first time the Google Bot visits your website, it will only look at the first page of your site. They do this to ensure that your site is legitimate when they come back in a few more days. When the bot returns, usually the next day, it will look through your site a little deeper. They continue this process until your entire site has been indexed—a process that can take up to six months.

When Google indexes your site, they look at tons of different variables to determine your site's page rank—these items include (but are not limited to) your site's domain name, a website's Title tag, h1 tags, and the first few paragraph tags. Other attributes Google takes into consideration are the website's response time, outside links pointing to your website, and which websites your own site links to.

Summary

Building a community website powered by WordPress is a snap thanks to BuddyPress. However, building the actual community is significantly harder. Take your time and expect the process to take months, if not years.

The basics of building a community, which we saw in this chapter, are as follows:

- BuddyPress features
- How to install BuddyPress
- BuddyPress themes
- BuddyPress plugins
- Driving traffic to your community

In the next chapter, you will learn about turning your blog into a cash register, or at least a steady stream of revenue, with tools such as Google Adwords, PayPal, Zazzle. com, and more.

6
Generating Revenue

In this chapter, we will cover the top plugins for turning your blog into a money-making machine, or at least to make enough money to buy yourself a beer or two. But keep in mind that it is possible to make a living from blogging; take techcrunch.com for example, which raked in over 2.7 million dollars in one year.

However, don't expect to become a millionaire overnight; instead you should expect to try out a few of these plugins to generating a little revenue and tweak your money-making strategies over time.

In this chapter, we will cover the following:

- Collecting donations with PayPal
- Promoting your art and design with Zazzle
- Automatically including Amazon-related products on a post
- Getting paid to promote music on your blog
- Working with Google AdSense
- Selling digital goods with your own shopping cart
- Invoicing clients
- Selling ad space on your site

Donation Can

By Jarkko Laine (http://jarkkolaine.com/)

- **Why it's awesome**: Public gauge of your current donations
- **Why it was picked**: Ease of use, goal tracking

- **License**: GNU General Public License
- **Manual Install URL**:
  http://wordpress.org/extend/plugins/donation-can/
- **Automatic Install search term**: Donation Can
- **Geek level**: Newbie
- **Configuration location**: **Top Navigation | Donation Can**
- **Used in**: Widget

Donation Can is your blogs PayPal tip-jar with a twist. Instead of just a little **Donate Now** button, like the plethora of other donation-based plugins, Donation Can makes reaching your donation goals a public affair.

The goal metaphor within Donation Can simply represents a financial objective for your donations. For example, one goal might be "Help Buy Me a Mac" with the goal target amount of $500. The Donation Can widget will display your goal's purpose and progress and a link to **Donate Now**. As readers donate, Donation Can tracks how close you get to your goal and displays a progress bar.

Donation Can also includes an Administrator Dashboard widget that gives a quick overview of your current goals and their status.

Fundraising Status

Latest Donations

No donations yet.

Goal Progress

New Computer	$ 0 / 500.00
TOTAL	**$ 0 / 500**

Using PayPal account: **printfu@gmail.com**

You are using **Donation Can (version 1.4.2)**. Check out the plugin home page for more information or to give feedback.

Donation Can is free software. The plugin was developed to support Train for Humanity, a non-profit organization aiming to promote humanity through everyday athletes' training efforts. Train for Humanity has now been closed, but if you find the plugin useful, consider donating to Habitat for Humanity's efforts to help in rebuilding Haiti.

(Change Settings) (Update Goals)

Zazzle Widget

By Rajesh Subramanian (http://www.rajesh.be/)

- **Why it's awesome**: Promote your own T-Shirt designs for free
- **Why it was picked**: Easy to install, you pick what to promote

- **License**: GNU General Public License
- **Manual Install URL**:
  `http://wordpress.org/extend/plugins/zazzle-widget/`
- **Automatic Install search term**: Zazzle Widget
- **Geek level**: Newbie
- **Configuration location**: None
- **Used in**: Widget

Zazzle.com is one of the leading "on-demand" clothing manufacturers. Your designs can be printed on t-shirts, hats, mouse pads, and countless other items. Heck, `Zazzle.com` can even print a photo of your cat on a pair of boxers—the options are limitless.

As people buy one of your products, you receive a commission. The commissions earned are based on how much over the standard price you set each of your items. For example, **Zazzle** requires that a white t-shirt costs $12.00, you can then price your design at $14.00; each time your shirt is purchased, you get $2.00. As you can see, the opportunity for making some serious money exists, if your designs are good enough and you drive enough traffic.

The Zazzle widget will dynamically pull in your Zazzle design and display them in your blogs sidebar. Optionally, you can display other products by keyword. However, you will not make any money from those referrals.

Setting up the Zazzle Widget

Unlike most plugins, the Zazzle Widget's configuration happens completely in the Widget's setting located in **Appearance | Widgets**. Once you have included the widget into your sidebar, you will see an array of options to configure.

The only required field within this setup is the **Zazzle Associate ID**. If you do not have a **Zazzle Associate ID**, you can sign up for one at http://www.zazzle. com/sell/tools/seller. If you want to help Rajesh (the plugin author), you can leave his **Zazzle Associate ID** alone; now he will earn a commission from any of the products you sell.

AmazonFeed

By Warkensoft Production (http://warkensoft.com/)

- **Why it's awesome**: Automatically finds products on Amazon that relate to your blog post
- **Why it was picked**: Super fast way of generating clicks and buys on your Amazon Affiliate account

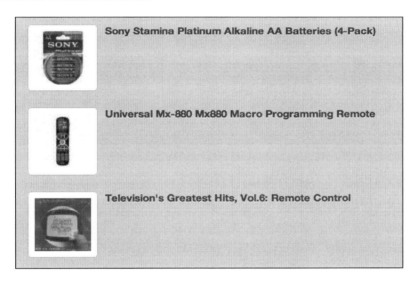

- **License**: GNU General Public License
- **Manual Install URL**:
  http://wordpress.org/extend/plugins/amazonfeed/
- **Automatic Install search term**: AmazonFeed
- **Geek level**: Webmaster
- **Configuration location: Tools | AmazonFeed**
- **Used in**: Pages, posts

AmazonFeed is a great way to include related Amazon products in blog posts or pages. To take advantage of the revenue stream, you will need to have an Amazon Web Service account, which can be obtained from `http://aws.amazon.com/`.

Setting up AmazonFeed

AmazonFeed does require a bit of setup to get it up and running; these settings are pretty self-explanatory. Once installed, you will find the AmazonFeed configuration located in the **Tools** navigation of your WordPress Admin. Once inside, you will see a message stating that AmazonFeed hasn't been set up yet; you can click this link to get directly where we need to go.

Configuration

1. Click the **Connection** tab

2. Provide your **AWS Access Key** and **AWS Private Key**. Both of these can be obtained from `https://aws-portal.amazon.com/gp/aws/developer/account/index.html`.

3. Provide your **Associate Id** located at `https://aws-portal.amazon.com/`.

After you have configured AmazonFeed, you are ultimately done with the required steps. Each time you create a new post or a new page, AmazonFeed will automatically include a list of related products at the bottom.

Post / page specific items

You can override the default settings on specific products on a page/post basis by using the module at the bottom of your edit post or edit page form. Within this module, you can define a specific keyword to search on Amazon, disable Amazon Product feed all-together, or change the default sort-order.

Advertising Manager

By Scott Switzer and Martin Fitzpatrick (`http://www.switzer.org/`)

- **Why it's awesome**: Easily add Google Ads to your blog
- **Why it was picked**: Popularity, update frequency, fairly easy to use

- **License**: GNU General Public License
- **Manual Install URL** : `http://wordpress.org/extend/plugins/advertising-manager/`
- **Automatic Install search term**: Advertising Manager
- **Geek level**: Webmaster
- **Configuration location: Top Navigation | Ads & Settings | Ads**
- **Used in**: Pages, posts, widgets

Google AdSense is the defacto advertising method on most websites and blogs today. With its targeted algorithm, AdSense will display ads that relate specifically to a blog post's content. If a reader is reading about your new houseboat, they will most likely be presented with ads about boating, houseboats, and water activities.

If you don't already have an AdSense account, you will need to create one by visiting `http://google.com/adsense`.

Creating a Google AdSense Ad

First you will need to create a Google AdSense Ad before you can include the ad on your website. After you have created your AdSense account, and within your AdSense homepage, click **AdSense Setup**.

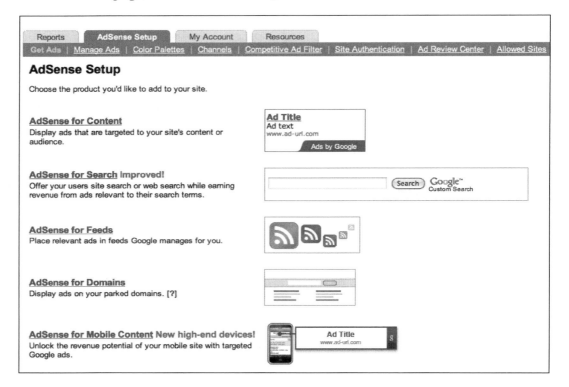

The following are the steps to creating a Google AdSense Ad:

1. **Choose an Ad Product**: AdSense offers many different formats to display ads, but for this plugin, we want to use **AdSense for Content**.

2. **Choose Ad Type**: AdSense offers two types of Ads for content—**Ad Unit** that contains text ads and/or image ads or **Link Unit** which displays a list of topics that are relevant to your website.

3. **Choose Ad Format and Color**: Select the size and format of your ad. If you are including this ad in your sidebar, you should only select an ad that is either equal to or smaller than the width of your sidebar. You can also define colors and fonts within this step.

4. **Choose Ad Channels**: An ad channel helps you track the performance of a specific ad unit. For example, you might create a channel called "My Blogs Sidebar" or "My Blogs Home Page"; you will then be able to report the effectiveness of your ads by these definitions.

5. **Save and Get Code**: Name your ad something helpful, and click **Submit** and **Get Code**.

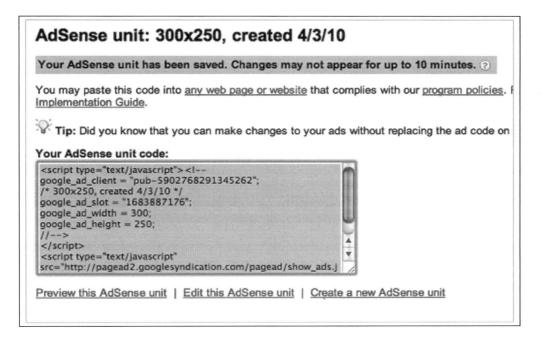

Creating your first ad in Advertising Manager

Now that we have the Google AdSense code, we have to add it to the Advertising Manager plugin. We start the process by clicking on **Ads | Create New** from within your blogs Administrator section.

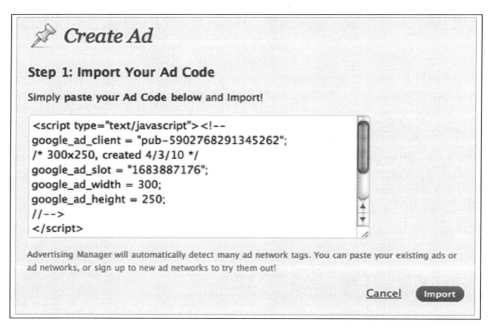

Paste your Google AdSense code into the textbox and click **Import**. Advertising Manager will automatically import all of your ad settings, including Account ID, Slot ID, and Ad Type. While I focus on Google AdSense with this plugin, you can also include ad code from other advertising networks.

Adding the Widget

In order to display your new Google Ads on your website, you will need to add the Advertising Manager Widget (called **Advertisement**) to your sidebar.

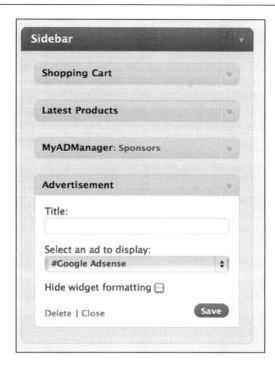

After you have included your Advertisement widget, you will need to select which Ad to display. The Ad to Display drop-down box will show you all of the different ads that you set up within the **Manage Your Advertising** section of the plugin.

iTunes Affiliate Link Maker (iTALM)

By Scott Switzer and Martin Fitzpatrick (http://www.switzer.org/)

- **Why it's awesome**: Makes adding "Purchase Song" links to your blog super simple
- **Why it was picked**: Fairly easy to use, ability to search iTunes from within WordPress

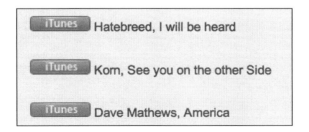

- **License**: GNU General Public License
- **Manual Install URL**: `http://wordpress.org/extend/plugins/itunes-affiliate-link-maker/`
- **Automatic Install search term**: iTunes Affiliate Link Maker
- **Geek level**: Webmaster
- **Configuration location**: **Settings | iTALM**
- **Used in**: Pages, posts

iTALM is an easy-to-use plugin that allows you to link directly to a song, album, or artist within the iTunes Store along with your iTunes Affiliate ID. While you do not need to be an iTunes Affiliate to use this plugin, you will need to set up one if you would like to cash in. To create an iTunes Affiliate Account, visit `http://www.apple.com/itunes/affiliates/`.

Adding links to a post

Click the **iTunes** icon on your editor's toolbar to insert an iTunes link to one of your posts or pages.

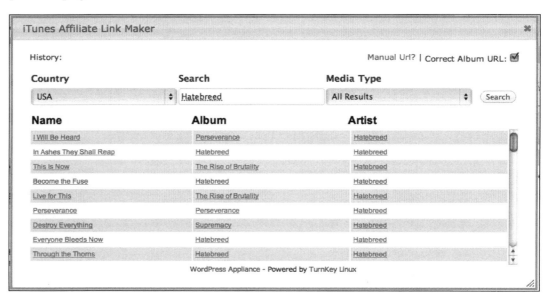

The iTunes Affiliate Link Maker will pop up a window that allows you to search the entire iTunes library of over 6 million songs. Once you find the artist, album, or song that you want to include, simply click the corresponding link.

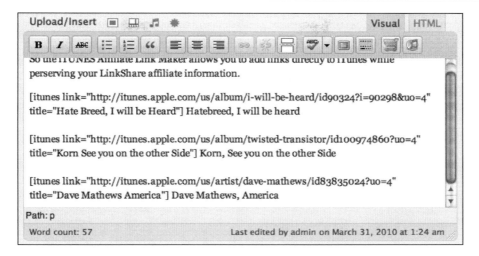

Anytime someone clicks one of your iTunes links, they will first be redirected to an iTunes page with more detail about the artist, song, or album. If the user has iTunes installed, the application will open up and be redirected to the specific song to be purchased. If the visitor doesn't have iTunes, they will be redirected to song's iTunes webpage.

WP e-Commerce, FREE Version

By Instinct.co.nz (http://www.instinct.co.nz/)

- **Why it's awesome**: Integrated e-commerce on your blog
- **Why it was picked**: Powerful settings, multiple credit processing options, lots of features

- **License**: GNU General Public License
- **Manual Install URL**:
  http://wordpress.org/extend/plugins/wp-e-commerce/
- **Automatic Install search term**: wp-ecommerce

- **Geek level**: Webmaster
- **Configuration location**: **Top Navigation | Products**
- **Used in**: Products, pages, posts, widgets

An entire book could be written on **WP e-Commerce** and all of its functionality. For the sake of brevity, this section will only cover a few of WP e-Commerce's features.

WP e-Commerce is a free plugin. However, the free version lacks some of the more advanced features that you might require if you plan on running a large e-commerce site from your blog.

The Gold Cart version costs $195.00 for companies and $40 for individuals and can be purchased at `http://getshopped.org`. This add-on includes:

- Grid view
- Multiple image upload
- Product searching
- Payment gateways for: Authorize.net, BluePay, and more

Setting up WP e-Commerce

WP e-Commerce does require a bit of initial setup. In this section, we will cover the bare requirements needed to sell a product online, but first you should make sure you have a PayPal account before you do anything else. Create a PayPal account at `http://paypal.com`.

Adding a digital product

In order to create your first product, visit your blog's Administrator section, and click on **Products | Products**.

Product Detail

First you will need to provide a **Product Name**, **Stock Keeping Unit (SKU)**, **Price**, and **Sale Price**.

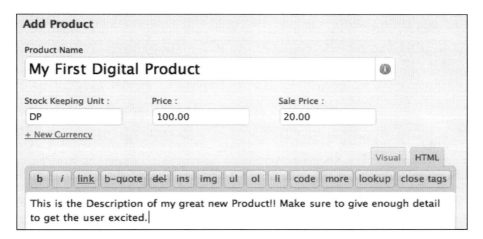

- Stock Keeping Unit or **SKU**: This is a short code that represents your product beyond a long product name
- Price: The price of the product
- Sales Price: The price of the product if it's on sale

Categories and Tags

Categories and Tags are a quick way of organizing your products into logical groups.

- Categories is a grouping or set of similar products
- Tag is a single word that, like a category, describes the product you are selling

Price and Stock Control

This section focuses on different configurations for pricing, taxes, and stock-on-hand.

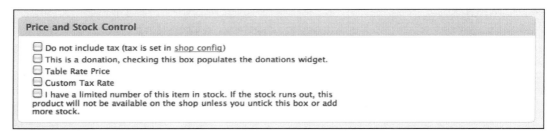

Shipping Details

WP e-Commerce also supports dynamic shipping prices based on the product's weight and the shipping carrier the visitor selected. WP e-Commerce supports integrated shipping lookups for FedEx, UPS, and USPS.

- **Weight**: The weight of the product is entered here.
- **Flat Rate Setting**: If you are not using the UPS or FedEx APIs, then you can set a specific cost for this Product's shipping
- **Disregard Shipping for this product**: If you are selling a digital good, then make sure this checkbox is checked

Product Images

Upload the photo of the product you want to display both in the "Grid" product view as well as on the **Product Detail** page. Unfortunately, **multiple product thumbnails** is only available if you purchase the Gold Cart module.

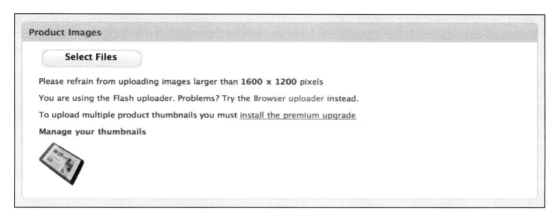

Once uploaded, your product image will automatically be included in the **Product List** view of your **Products Page**, as shown in the following screenshot:

Product Download

If you are selling a digital good, this is where you will define the file that the user will be able to download, once they have checked out. WP e-Commerce's download links are dynamic for the purchase, which kills the ability of the visitor to share the download link with other people.

Setting up your Payment Gateway

A **Payment Gateway** is the method used to connect to companies that can accept money on your behalf, for example, PayPal.

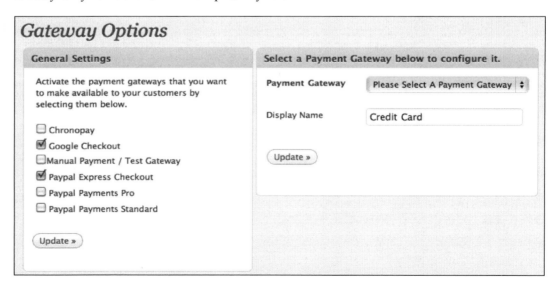

You should, at a minimum, use PayPal to collect payment and avoid collecting credit cards on your own! Unless you plan on having a secure site and a dedicated resource that can ensure that your website's security is continually up-to-date, storing credit cards on your own is usually a bad idea.

Web Invoice—invoicing and billing for WordPress

By SH Mohanjith (http://mohanjith.com/)

- **Why it's awesome**: Manage and send invoices directly from WordPress
- **Why it was picked**: Easy to use, just enough power, subscription-based invoices

Invoice From:

Listy.m

1234 Pine View Dr,
Carmel Indiana 46040

317-555-5555

Tax ID: 1234-123-123123

Item	Cost
Hosting	$12.00
Hours of Support	$12.00
Tax (7%)	$1.68
Invoice Total:	**$25.68**

- **License**: GNU General Public License
- **Manual Install URL**: http://wordpress.org/extend/plugins/web-invoice/
- **Automatic Install search term**: Web Invoice
- **Geek level**: Newbie
- **Configuration location: Top Navigation | Products**
- **Used in**: Invoices

Web Invoice is an indispensable plugin for anyone who currently bills clients or offers any type of subscription service. Out of the box, Web Invoice supports one time payment invoices via PayPal.

To leverage Web Invoice's recurring billing feature, you will need to have either a PayPal Business or PayPal Payflow account. You can also leverage some other services such as MerchantPlus, MerchantExpress.com, or MerchantWarehouse. However, as I have never used these services, I can't reliably confirm if they work or not.

Web Invoice sends invoices via e-mail and includes a link that will redirect the client back to an online view of your invoice. Once the client reviews and approves the invoice, they can click the Pay Now link that will take them directly to PayPal.

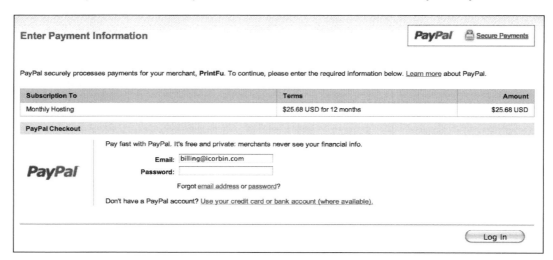

Setting up an invoice

To create a new invoice, click **New Invoice** from the Web Invoice top-level navigation box within your WordPress administrator.

Select the client

Web Invoice uses your WordPress users as potential clients to bill by displaying all of the current users in a drop-down box. If your client is not present, simply click the "Create a new user account" link and complete the **Add New User** form.

Client Information

As WordPress does not collect address, company, and shipping information, you will need to complete the additional fields within the **Client Information** box. This step will only need to be performed once as Web Invoice will store this information next time you want to bill the same client.

Recurring Billing

In order to set up **Recurrent Billing**, you will need to click the "Create a recurring billing schedule for this invoice" link.

- **Subscription Name**: This is the name of your subscription that will be displayed to the user when they are redirected to PayPal. For example, "Monthly Hosting" or eZine Monthly Subscription.

- **Start Date**: You have the option of either starting the subscription immediately or starting it at a future date. To set a future date, you will need to click the **Specify Start Date** link and provide the specific starting date.

- **Bill Every**: This field allows you to define how often this subscription will be billed. For example, you might provide 2 in the first input-box and select **month(s)** from the drop-down box in order to bill this client every two months.

- **Total Billing Cycles**: You can choose how long this subscription service will be active by including the number of times to bill. For example, if you selected to bill every two months, and if you have six billing cycles, then your total subscription time will be 12 months.

Invoice Details

- **Subject**: Provide a high-level overview of the purpose of this invoice. Additionally, the subject field will also be used as the main subject of the e-mail sent to your client.

- **Description/PO**: Use the Description/PO field to offer more details about the invoice. The more detailed it is, the better.

- **Itemized List**: Provide the name, description, quantity of items, and the unit price for each individual item. For example, Name: Monthly Hosting, Quantity: 1, Unit Price: $5.99.

Publish

- **Invoice ID**: By default, Web Invoice will generate a unique Invoice ID, but you can set a custom one by clicking the "Custom Invoice ID" link.

- **Tax**: Make sure you check with your State's tax requirements to know what Percentage (if any) is required for the types of items you are selling.

- **Currency**: Change the dollar type required to pay.

- **Due Date**: Determine when the invoice is due, you can subsequently pick from the clickable links for "In One Week" or "In 30 Days".

My Ad Manager

By Michael (visionmasterdesigns.com)

- **Why it's awesome**: Sell ad space on your blog directly to visitors
- **Why it was picked**: Easy to use, you retain 100 percent of the sale

- **License**: GNU General Public License
- **Manual Install URL**: `http://wordpress.org/extend/plugins/web-invoice/`
- **Automatic Install search term**: Web Invoice
- **Geek level**: Newbie
- **Configuration location**: **Top Navigation | Products**
- **Used in**: Invoices

Companies like BuySellAds.com have made it pretty easy for you to allow outside individuals and companies to buy **AD Space** on your website. **My Ad Manager** offers the same functionality without the need for a third party. Out of the box, My Ad Manager gives you the ability to create a "Buy an Ad" on one of your WordPress pages, which allows anyone to purchase advertising from your blog using PayPal.

Creating the Advertise Here Page

In order to allow visitors to purchase **AD Space**, you will first need to create a new page on your WordPress blog. This page should be called something like **Advertise Here** or "Place an Ad". All that is required for this page is the inclusion of My Ad Manager's custom tag.

Adding the Widget

To include the ads on your website, you will need to drag the My Ad Manager Widget to your blog's sidebar (**Appearance | Widgets**).

Setting up your House Ads

Unfortunately, this plugin does not default to the standard **Advertise Here** 125x125 ads. Instead, you will need to create your own Advertise Here links and include them as "Home" ads.

The following are the steps to setting up your House Ads:

1. Click the **My Ad Manager** from the top-level navigation.
2. Scroll down to the **Add Ad** section.
3. Create a name for your Ad like "Home Ad 1".
4. Provide the URL of the **Advertise Here** button; for a selection of free ads, use any of the URLs from the images that follow the screen shot.
5. Use the URL to the page you set up in the **Creating the Advertising Here** page, as shown in the last screen shot.
6. Set the duration of the Ad, which will default to one week.
7. Make sure Home is selected as the Type of Ad.
8. Click the **Add Ad** button.

To help you understand, I spent some time creating a handful of 125x125 Advertise Here ads, seen in the following screen shot. Simply visit the URL beneath each Ad block to download the corresponding AD-Image.

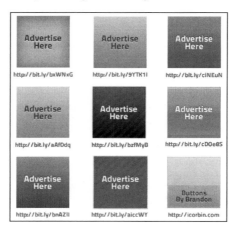

To see these buttons in color, visit `http://bit.ly/cctd46`.

Summary

In this chapter, we covered only a few of the ways to generate cash from your blogging activities. These included the following:

- Donation Can — An easy way to collect donations via PayPal
- Zazzle Widget — Promotes your Zazzle Store
- Amazon Feed — Includes related Amazon products for posts and pages
- Advertising Manager — Includes AdSense and other ad-network ads in your blog
- iTunes Affiliate Link Maker — Links directly to iTunes songs, artists, and albums
- WP e-Commerce — A full-fledged e-commerce platform built on WordPress
- Web Invoice — Invoicing and billing for WordPress
- My Ad Manager — Sell ads directly from your blog

In the next chapter, we will cover plugins for working with and promoting multiple authors or reporters.

7
Working with Multiple Authors

Nothing helps build a powerful online blog brand more than a horde of talented writers to contribute their ideas and content. In this chapter, we will cover a bunch of plugins that make working with multiple authors easy, efficient, and effective.

In this chapter, we cover:

- How to promote your authors
- How to track an author's performance
- How to add newsroom-worthy workflow processes
- How to track and limit functionality to different roles
- How to pretend you have more authors than you really do
- How to share advertising revenue with your authors

Authors Widget

By Gavriel Fleischer (`http://blog.fleischer.hu/gavriel/`)

- **Why it's awesome**: It's more practical than awesome, simply promote your authors
- **Why it was picked**: Popularity, ease of use

- **License**: GNU General Public License
- **Manual Install URL**: `http://wordpress.org/extend/plugins/authors/`
- **Automatic Install search term**: Authors Widget
- **Geek level**: Newbie
- **Configuration location**: None
- **Used in**: Widget

Authors Widget displays each of your authors, a link to their profile, and a link to an RSS feed containing only their posts. Once installed, you simply visit the **Appearance | Widgets** page and drag the **Authors Widget** to your sidebar.

Once inside of your sidebar, expand the widget to set the following customizations:

- Title—The text to show above the list of authors, which would be a good starting point.
- Format—It is either a list or a drop down. It's recommended to go with a list, as it helps the search engine bots find all of your juicy content. To a bot, a drop down is ultimately invisible.
- Order by Name or Post Count—Choosing **Post Count** will show the most type-happy authors first, which, in some cases, can cause a good/bad competition between authors. Going with name would be the politically correct way to go.
- Show Avatar—An avatar is simply a cute name for **Your picture**.
- Avatar Size—The pixel size of the author's photo. Consider staying between 32 pixels and 64 pixels, as these are the most common avatar sizes used today.
- Show RSS links—Toggle between showing and hiding a link for RSS feed containing only the author's posts. Make sure to tell your authors to promote their personal RSS feed to as many people as possible.
- Show post counts—This will show the number of posts an author has.
- Exclude Admin—Toggle between showing and hiding the admin account in the list. Personally, I suggest that you turn this feature off to ensure that you're not promoting your admin users' accounts publicly.
- Hide Credit—Turn on or off your support to Gavriel Fleischer, the plugin's author. If turned on, under your list of authors will be a link back to the plugin's home page.

Author Spotlight

By Debashish Chakrabarty (`http://www.debashish.com/`)

- **Why it's awesome**: Displays an author card on all posts written by the author
- **Why it was picked**: Simple widget, easy to use

- **License**: GNU General Public License
- **Manual Install URL**:
  `http://wordpress.org/extend/plugins/author-profile/`
- **Automatic Install search term**: Author Spotlight
- **Geek level**: Newbie
- **Configuration location**: None
- **Used in**: Widget

Author Spotlight is another truly simple plugin to promote your blog's most valuable assets, namely, its authors. Just as with any other widget-based plugin, you will need to visit **Appearance | Widgets** and drag the **Author Spotlight** widget to your blog's sidebar.

Styling the Author widget

Widgets often fall victim to a theme's stylesheet, meaning that the theme often ignores applying any type of styling to plugins that the original theme designer didn't intend on being used. Author Spotlight is no exception.

If you're an advanced user who's comfortable with CSS, here are the classes and IDs needed to restyle the default Author widget:

```css
#post_author_profile {
    font-size: 12px; font-family: Helvetica, Arial; margin:5px;
        padding:7px; background-color:#fff; border:solid 1px #ccc;
}
#post_author_profile h2 {
    margin:0px 0; padding:0; font-size:9px; text-transform: uppercase;
}
#post_author_profile h4 {
    font-size:20px; padding:0px; margin:3px 0;
}
#post_author_profile img.avatar {
    padding:5px; background-color:#fff; margin:5px 0px; border:solid
        1px #ccc;
}
#post_author_profile #author_profile {
    font-size:12px; line-height:14px; color:#666; margin:5px 0 5px;
}
#post_author_profile a {
    font-size:12px;
}
#post_author_profile > b {
    display:none;
}
```

Blog Metrics

By Joost de Valk (http://yoast.com/)

- **Why it's awesome**: Quick view of your authors' activities
- **Why it was picked**: Simplicity, accuracy

Author stats

brandon

Raw Author Contribution
3 posts per month
Avg: 206 words per post
Std dev: 301 words

Conversation Rate Per Post
Avg: 0.7 comments
Avg: 10 words in comments
Avg: 0 trackbacks

Full Stats
Posts: 3
Words in posts: 618
Comments: 2
Words in comments: 32
Trackbacks: 0
Months blogging: 1

Brandon Corbin

Raw Author Contribution
posts per month

Conversation Rate Per Post
Avg: 0 comments
Avg: 0 trackbacks

Full Stats
Posts: 0
Words in posts: 0
Comments: 0
Words in comments: 0
Trackbacks: 0
Months blogging: 6

patrick

Raw Author Contribution
1 post per month
Avg: 284 words per post

Conversation Rate Per Post
Avg: 0 comments
Avg: 0 trackbacks

Full Stats
Posts: 1
Words in posts: 284
Comments: 0
Words in comments: 0
Trackbacks: 0
Months blogging: 1

- **License**: GNU General Public License
- **Manual Install URL**:
  http://wordpress.org/extend/plugins/blog-metrics
- **Automatic Install search term**: Blog Metrics
- **Geek level**: Newbie
- **Configuration location: Settings | Blog Metrics**
- **Used in**: Post editor

Keeping tabs on your author's work is never a bad thing. **Blog Metrics** gives you a snapshot of each of your author's performance, ranging from posts per month, number of posts, total comments, number of words per post, and total trackbacks.

Cimy User Extra Fields

By Marco Cimmino (http://www.marcocimmino.net/)

- **Why it's awesome**: Lets you create additional profile fields for your authors
- **Why it was picked**: Adds infinite possibilities to user profile pages

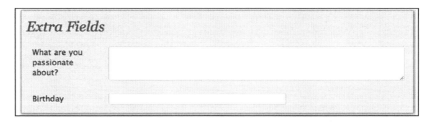

Extra Fields

What are you passionate about?

Birthday

- **License**: GNU General Public License
- **Manual Install URL**:
  `http://wordpress.org/extend/plugins/cimy-user-extra-fields`
- **Automatic Install search term**: CIMY User Extra Fields
- **Geek level**: Webmaster
- **Configuration location**: **Settings | CIMY User Extra Fields**
- **Used in**: Author profiles

The **Cimy User Extra Fields** plugin extends the default profile provided by WordPress, giving you the ability to collect additional information on each of your members. For example, you might want to add a Twitter username or Facebook profile URL to help promote your author's other social activities.

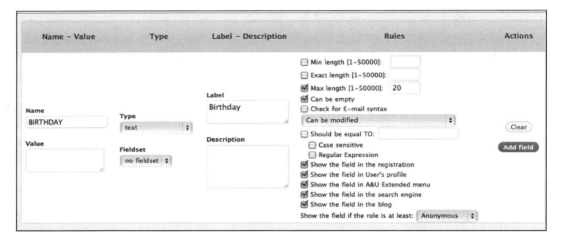

Pre-Publish Reminder

By Nick Ohrn (`http://plugin-developer.com/`)

- **Why it's awesome**: Helps authors remember specific tasks before they publish
- **Why it was picked**: Simple, easy to install, straightforward interface

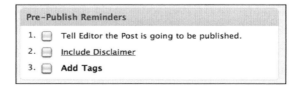

- **License**: GNU General Public License

- **Manual Install URL**:
  `http://wordpress.org/extend/plugins/pre-publish-reminders/`
- **Automatic Install search term**: Pre-Publish Reminder
- **Geek level**: Newbie
- **Configuration location**: **Tools | Publish Reminder**
- **Used in**: Post Editor

Pre-Publish Reminder is one of those simple plugins that you quickly realize is invaluable. Many times, you have a customized workflow you try to follow when creating a new post, for example, **Add an Image** or **Link to Related Articles**. Unless you have those rules written down, there's a very likely chance that you will completely forget them. This is where Pre-Publish Reminder comes in.

This plugin allows you to create a simple task list containing different steps you need to complete before you publish. Once an item is completed, you simply check the checkbox and the state will be remembered. Alternatively, you can uncheck your tasks in the case of an accidental click. It's good to know that this plugin will not stop you from posting—it's purely a reminder.

Edit Flow

By Batmoo, Daniel Bachhuber, sbressler, Andrew Spittle (`http://editflow.org`)

- **Why it's awesome**: Custom post statuses, workflow control, and expanded user roles
- **Why it was picked**: Flexibility to match your own workflow

Name	Description	# of Posts
Assigned	The post has been assigned to a writer	0
Draft	Post is simply a draft	1
Pending Review	The post needs to be reviewed by an Editor	0
Pitch	Post idea proposed	0
Waiting for Feedback	The post has been sent to the editor, and is waiting on feedback	0
Name	Description	Posts

- **License**: GNU General Public License
- **Manual Install URL**: http://wordpress.org/extend/plugins/edit-flow
- **Automatic Install search term**: Edit Flow
- **Geek level**: Webmaster
- **Configuration location**: **Top Navigation | Edit Flow**
- **Used in**: Administrator, posts

Edit Flow enables a multi-author blog environment to handle more of the editorial workflow than what WordPress offers by default. With Edit Flow, an editor can assign a post to any author. Authors can submit a post for review and even pitch an idea to an editor.

Edit Flow also allows you to define your own custom workflow statuses that can be tweaked to meet your current editorial process. These custom statuses will be available to authors to set a blog post into states like **Waiting for Review** or **Ready for Editing**.

Once installed, Edit Flow will create a few new **User Groups** that more closely match those of a traditional newsroom. These new groups include:

- **Copy Editors** — Those who correct and proofread posts
- **Photographers** — Those who take the pretty pictures
- **Reporters** — Those who actually write the articles
- **Sales Team** — Those who try to sell
- **Section Editors** — Those who define what should be covered, and who should be covering it
- **Web Team** — Those who help with technical issues

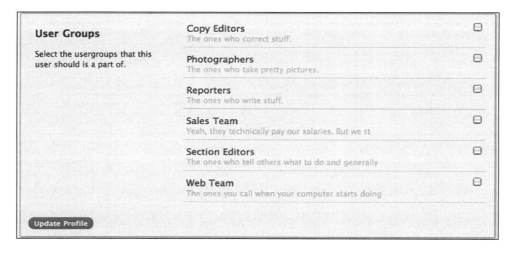

Audit Trail

By John Godley (http://urbangiraffe.com/)

- **Why it's awesome**: Keeps track of who's doing what on your blog
- **Why it was picked**: Easy to use, tracks user by IP

Bulk Actions ⬍ (Apply)	25 per-page ⬍ (Filter)			*Displaying 1–4 of 4*
☐ **User**	**Action**	**Target**	**Date** △	**IP**
☐ admin	Save page	46	April 4, 2010 00:40	192.168.32.1
☐ admin	Save page	38	April 4, 2010 00:40	192.168.32.1
☐ admin	Save page	21	April 4, 2010 00:40	192.168.32.1
☐ admin	Save page	45	April 4, 2010 00:40	192.168.32.1
☐ **User**	**Action**	**Target**	**Date** △	**IP**

- **License**: GNU General Public License
- **Manual Install URL**:
  http://wordpress.org/extend/plugins/audit-trail
- **Automatic Install search term**: Audit Trail
- **Geek level**: Webmaster
- **Configuration location: Tools | Audit Trail**
- **Used in**: Administrator

Audit Trail helps you keep track of specific events that happen on your blog. Each action is recorded in Audit Trail's logs with the username, time of event, IP address, the action taken, and the results of the action. Logging is available for:

- **File attachments** — When someone uploads a new image or file
- **Category management** — When someone adds, edits, or deletes a category
- **Comment management** — When a comment is added or modified
- **Link management** — When a user modifies a link
- **Post & page management** — When any action happens on a post or a page
- **Theme switching** — When a user switches a theme
- **User profile & logins** — When users update their profiles or log in
- **User page visits** — Every time a user visits your blog; if your website gets a lot of traffic, leave this turned off

WP-CMS Post Control

By Jonnyauk (http://jonnya.net/)

- **Why it's awesome**: Adds an additional level of control and security based on an author's role

- **Why it was picked**: Easiest to install, is a must needed functionality

- **License**: GNU General Public License
- **Manual Install URL**:
  http://wordpress.org/extend/plugins/wp-cms-post-control
- **Automatic Install search term**: WP-CMS Post Control
- **Geek level**: Webmaster
- **Configuration location: Tools | Post Control**
- **Used in**: Posts, pages, comments, and authors

When dealing with multiple authors, you do have to be aware of who has what access, and which users can do what within your blog. **WP-CMS Post Control** gives you the power to define specifically what types of users have what types of access.

Currently, the plugin supports control over the following items:

Page controls

- Attributes—Define who can modify page attributes
- Author—Defines who can change the current author of a page
- Custom Fields—Define who can modify custom fields
- Discussion—Defines who can modify discussion settings
- Revisions—Define who can work with different page revisions

Post controls

- Author—Defines who can change the current author of a post
- Categories—Define who can modify post categories
- Comments—Define who can modify comments for a post
- Custom Fields—Define who can modify custom fields
- Discussion—Defines who can modify discussion settings
- Revisions—Define who can work with different page revisions
- Tags—Define who can modify a post's tags
- Trackbacks—Define who can modify trackback settings

Guest Blogger

By Bob King (http://wealthynetizen.com/)

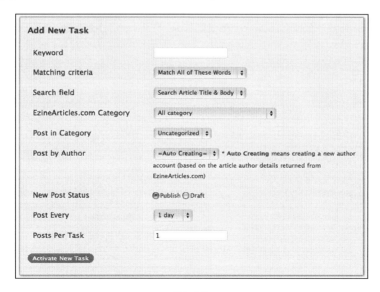

- **License**: GNU General Public License
- **Manual Install URL**:
  `http://wordpress.org/extend/plugins/guest-blogger`
- **Automatic Install search term**: Guest Blogger
- **Geek level**: Webmaster
- **Configuration location**: **Tools | Guest Blogger**
- **Used in**: Posts

Guest Blogger is a great way to continually fill your blog with relevant content, without ever having to work with an author. Guest Blogger pulls content from `http://ezinearticles.com`, a repository of free-to-republish articles covering topics like *Female Libido Boosters* and *Time Management* plus everything in between. The content is usually accurate, timely, and written in an internet-acceptable grammar—a great filler for a lackluster news day.

Of course, nothing is truly free and EzineArticles is no exception. Part of the **Terms of Service** requires you to leave the article intact, including the footer that contains a link back to EzineArticles website. Additional terms and conditions can be read at `http://ezinearticles.com/terms-of-service.html`.

 EzineArticles allows only up to 25 articles to be republished each year per domain, up to 10 domains.

Adding a new article import

Visit **Settings | Guest Blogger** and scroll down to the **Add a Task** section. The **Add a Task** form is there to let you customize the types of articles you want to import.

- Keyword—Include only articles that contain a specific keyword.
- Matching Criteria—How strict should the search be while looking for articles with the keyword defined above.
- Search Field—Which parts should be searchable.
- EzineArticles.com Category—Select to pull from a specific category of articles.
- Post in Category—The category on your blog to post the new articles.
- Post by Author—You can manually define a specific author account to post under, or guest blogger will automatically create a new account for the author who actually wrote the article.

- New Post Status—Go with "Draft" so you can preview the articles before they are pushed to your public website.

- Post Every—How many days to go between running this importer? Keep in mind, according to EzineArticles's **Terms and Conditions**, you may only republish upto 25 articles in a calendar year.

- Posts per Task—The number of articles you want imported each time it's run.

Once you have completed the form, click **Activate New Task**, after which your task will be added to the guest blogger queue—**Active Posting Tasks**.

Active Posting Tasks

Keyword	Next Update	Matching criteria/ Search Field/ Category	Post Category	Author	Interval	Status	Posts Per Task	Last Posts	Total Posts	Delete	Check Articles	Post Now
computer	14 Apr 00:49	All/ Title&Body/ All category	Printing	=Auto=	1days	publish	5	5	5	Delete	Check	Post

You have posted **5** posts(publish/draft). Clear counter

Last operation status: **Success: Article retrieved and posted.**

Last scheduled operation: **Tue Apr 13 0:41:04 UTC 2010**

Subscribe to Author Posts Feed

By Ruben Sargsyan (`http://rubensargsyan.com/`)

- **Why it's awesome**: Promotes your authors, allows authors to promote their posts

- **Why it was picked**: Plug and play

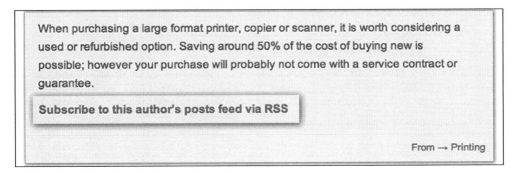

When purchasing a large format printer, copier or scanner, it is worth considering a used or refurbished option. Saving around 50% of the cost of buying new is possible; however your purchase will probably not come with a service contract or guarantee.

Subscribe to this author's posts feed via RSS

From → Printing

- **License**: GNU General Public License
- **Manual Install URL**:
  `http://wordpress.org/extend/plugins/subscribe-to-author-posts-feed`
- **Automatic Install search term**: Subscribe to Author Posts Feed
- **Geek level**: Newbie
- **Configuration location**: None
- **Used in**: Posts

Subscribe to Author Posts Feed helps promote each of your blogger's articles. This simple plugin does exactly as the name specifies and creates a link at the bottom of each article to the author's RSS feed.

Author Advertising

By Harley Quine (`http://www.harleyquine.com/`)

- **Why it's awesome**:
- **Why it was picked**:

- **License**: GNU General Public License
- **Manual Install URL**: `http://wordpress.org/extend/plugins/author-advertising-plugin/`

- **Automatic Install search term**: Author Advertising Plugin
- **Geek level**: Webmaster
- **Configuration location**: Settings | Author Advertising Config
- **Used in**: Posts, widget

You can't deny that money is a good motivator, especially for starving bloggers, but paying authors is a time consuming costly task. Instead, why not let Google pay them? **Author Advertising Plugin** allows your guest bloggers the ability to capture some of your website's Google advertising juice by rotating ads throughout your website with your Google AdSense account and your author's Google AdSense account.

You'll need have a good understanding of Google AdSense to be able to leverage this plugin. You can read about Google AdSense in *Chapter 6, Generating Revenue*, but at the bare minimum, you need to have a Google AdSense account from `http://google.com/adsense`.

For this example, we are going to make the following assumptions:

1. You have a Google AdSense account.
2. We are only going to offer the widget advertising space.
3. Your blog's sidebar is between 150 px and 350 px wide.
4. You've setup a new Google AdSense ad spot that fits your sidebar, and you have already copied the snippet of JavaScript Google requires you to include on your website.

Setting up Author Advertising widget

Setting up this plugin does seem a bit overly complex. However, the results are well worth it. To get started, visit **Settings | Author Advertising Config**.

- Admin Advertising ID—This should be your Google Publisher ID. Your Publisher ID is located at `https://www.google.com/adsense` in the upper-right-hand corner of the screen.

- Admin Percentage—This is the percentage of ads that should be purely owned by your AdSense account.

- Lowest User Level—Define what types of users should be able to include their AdSense Publisher ID.

- Random Home—Pick a user's Publisher ID at random every time the home page is visited (this would be a nice gesture).

The Author Page

The Author Page is a new page your blog members will be able to access to provide their own AdSense Publisher ID.

- **Title** — The name of the Author Page, for example, **My Advertising Setup**.

- **Page Content** — A message to your users explaining how your revenue sharing is set up and any other customized message you would like to show to the user.

- **Custom Fields** — Outside of the scope of this book. These fields will be used if you want to start adding different advertising networks or additional parameters to pass to an ad call.

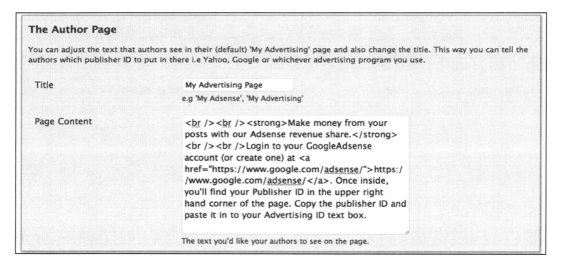

Advertising code

For the purpose of this book, we will only cover the very last Ad space, namely, **Author Advertising Widget**. Simply deselect **Active for Ad Place 1, 2, 3 and 4**. If you have never dealt with a template before, things might get a little confusing in the next step, but hang with it! You need to paste the Ad Code from Google AdSense in the **Author Advertising Widget** textbox.

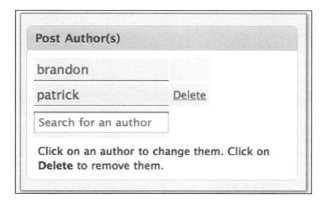

Widget: The Author Advertising widget.

Once you have pasted the code into the textbox, you will need to replace your Publisher ID (located in the second line of the code above) with %pubid%. When the widget is loaded, the %pubid% will be automatically filled in with either your ID or one of your users. Pretty cool huh?

Co-Author Plus

By Mohammad Jangda (http://digitalize.ca/)

- **Why it's awesome**: Allows multiple authors to get credit for a single blog post
- **Why it was picked**: Popularity and stability

Post Author(s)

brandon

patrick   Delete

Search for an author

Click on an author to change them. Click on **Delete** to remove them.

- **License**: GNU General Public License
- **Manual Install URL**:
  http://wordpress.org/extend/plugins/co-authors-plus/
- **Automatic Install search term**: Co-Authors Plus
- **Geek level**: WPNinja

- **Configuration location**: Settings | Co-Authors Plus
- **Used in**: Posts

By default, WordPress doesn't offer the ability to show if multiple authors co-wrote a post. **Co-Authors Plus** fixes this lack of functionality by fixing the **Post Author(s)** module and a snippet of PHP that will need to be included on your **SinglePost** page.

In order to include your multiple author by-line, you will need to modify your theme. While this does require a little tinkering, the results are well worth it.

1. Go to the **Theme editor** by clicking **Appearance | Editor**.
2. Click **Single Post** (single.php) from the list of available pages located on the right side of the page.
3. Inside of the big text area, look for <?php the_author_posts_link(); ?>. This snippet of code is what's responsible for generating the current by-line on your site.
4. Replace the previous snippet of code with the following code snippet.
5. Click **Update File.**

```
<? if(function_exists('coauthors_posts_links')) {
    coauthors_posts_links();
  } else {
    the_author_posts_link();
  }
?>
```

The last snippet of code will generate a new by-line containing each post's authors, as seen in the following image:

Private Messages for WordPress

By Rilwil (`http://hontap.blogspot.com/`)

- **Why it's awesome**: Author collaboration!

- **Why it was picked**: Functionality, popularity, and built-in archiving of messages

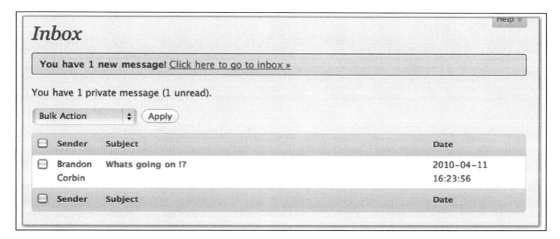

- **License**: GNU General Public License

- **Manual Install URL**: `http://wordpress.org/extend/plugins/private-messages-for-wordpress/`

- **Automatic Install search term**: Private Messages for WordPress

- **Geek level**: Newbie

- **Configuration location: Settings | Private Messages**

- **Used in**: Administrator

Private Messages for WordPress fills a massive gap within WordPress—interblog communications. Private Messages is essentially a mailbox within WordPress that allows communication between different authors and members of your blog.

Summary

Controlling a multi-author blog can be a challenge, but with the right tools, it can result in an incredibly powerful online brand.

- Authors Widget—Promotes your authors with this simple plugin
- Authors Spotlight—Showcases an author's bio on each of their stories
- Blog Metrics—Keeping track of your bloggers performance
- Cimy User Extra Fields—Extends the default WordPress profile
- Pre-Publish Reminder—Reminds yourself of tasks before you post
- Edit Flow—Adds powerful editing workflow to your blog
- Audi Trail—Tracks virtually every action that happens on your blog
- WP CMS Post Control—Defines who can do what within WordPress
- Guest Blogger—Automatically pulls content from `EzineArticles.com`
- Subscribe to Author Posts Feed—Promotes your author's RSS feeds
- Author Advertising—Shares advertising revenue with your authors
- Co-Author Plus—Adds co-authoring functionality to WordPress
- Private Messages for WordPress—Adds private messaging between your blog users

In the next chapter, you'll learn how to make backups of your blog and ensure that your site's security.

8
Security and Maintenance

Imagine waking up one morning to find that a hacker has taken down your site, or that one blog post went viral last night and now your website has crashed from the flood of traffic.

In this chapter, we'll cover the best plugins for ensuring that your blog is secure, the database is running optimally, and in the case of an emergency, you have a full backup copy of your blog.

In this chapter, we cover the following:

- How to protect your website from common hacking practices
- How to virtually eliminate comment spam
- How to make sure your blog is healthy
- How to back up your database and the entire blog
- How to make your website-screaming fast
- How to know when errors happen

Security basics

The first rule of Website Security is this: if a hacker wants to get into your website, he will. However, you don't have to make it easy for them, and hopefully, with enough safe-guards in place, the hacker will give up and move to his next victim.

In regards to WordPress, most successful hack attempts happen thanks to one of three things—a guessable password, an outdated WordPress install, or an outdated plugin.

Passwords

Instead of a short password like FlyLover use a short sentence like this: iAmAwesomeToday.

I also recommend that you make your password something, well, horribly negative; for example, "IAmStupidAndSmellFunny". The more awful and self-loathing, the better. Think about it, if someone ever asks for your password, you'll really stop and think about ever saying it out loud.

 Never use same password for your WordPress login and your database. If a hacker gets access to your database, they get access to everything, including the ability to execute server-side code on your website.

Update often

Update WordPress EVERY TIME a new version is released; no questions asked. Simply updating is the easiest way to deter potential hackers. Update plugins EVERY TIME a new version is released. Most of the hackers use known security holes in plugins to take over your blog.

Back up often

Back up as often as you possibly can. The web is still fragile, and your website will go down. Backing up is so easy that there is absolutely no excuse for "not doing it".

Limit Login Attempts

By Johan Eenfeldt (`http://devel.kostdoktorn.se/`)

- **Why it's awesome**: Blocks hackers from trying countless username and passwords after a small number of failed attempts
- **Why it was picked**: An easy step to help your site from getting hacked

- **Manual Install URL**:
  http://WordPress.org/extend/plugins/limit-login-attempts/
- **Automatic Install search term**: Limit Login Attempts
- **Geek level**: Newbie
- **Configuration location: Settings | Limit Login Attempts**
- **Used in**: Administrator

It's fairly easy to write a program that continually tries to log in to your blog by running through every possible combination of common passwords. **Limit Login Attempts** makes this task completely pointless by locking out users (or bots) that incorrectly try to log in multiple times.

Setting up Limit Login Attempts

Limit Login Attempts doesn't require any additional setup or configuration beyond just installing and activating the plugin. However, if you want to tweak the default settings, head over to **Settings | Limit Login Attempts**.

Lockout

Allowed Retries—The total number of incorrect login attempts before the user is locked out.

Minutes lockout—The number of minutes the user will be banned from trying to log in again after N number of failed login attempts.

Handle cookie login—Determines if the lockout should be based on the user's IP address or cookies; it's recommended to stick with cookies, as IP addresses might be shared between multiple users.

Notify on lockout—Can be configured to log the IP address of the offending attempts and/or send an e-mail to the admin of your blog, notifying that a user has been locked out.

Secure WordPress

By Michael Torbert (`http://semperfiwebdesign.com/`)

- **Why it's awesome**: Makes it harder for hackers to know that your website is actually powered by WordPress

- **Why it was picked**: Easy to use and set up, and a fast way to limit risk

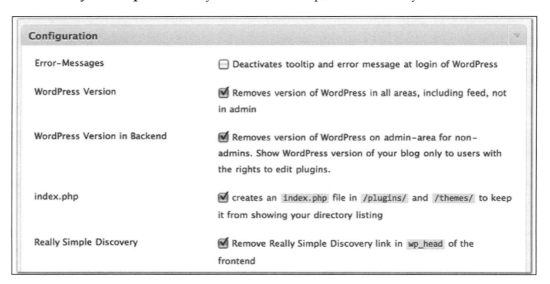

- **Manual Install URL**:
  `http://WordPress.org/extend/plugins/secure-WordPress/`

- **Automatic Install search term**: Secure WordPress
- **Geek level**: Newbie
- **Configuration location**: **Settings | Secure WP**
- **Used in**: Administrator

Out of the box, WordPress includes some features that are less than secure. **Secure WordPress** focuses on helping you fix these default settings to ensure that your blog isn't easily compromised.

Secure WordPress's options explained

The Secure WordPress's options can be explained as follows:

- Error messages—Deactivates tooltip and error messages at login of WordPress.

- WordPress version—Hides all instances of which version of WordPress you're running.

- WordPress version in Backend—Removes all instances of the version of WordPress to the Administrator section. This could cause issues with many plugins, if hidden.

- index.php—Creates an index file in both the plugins and theme directories. This index file will ensure that no one can see the individual files listed in the plugins and theme folders.

- Really Simple Discovery—This is a great method for other websites to learn about your blog and how to interact with it. However, this feature also exposes some information that hackers could take advantage of. If you run a high profile website, I would suggest that you disable **Really Simple Discovery**; otherwise, you should be ok leaving this feature enabled.

- Windows Live Writer—This option will remove the Windows Live Writer service that is running by default. If you're not using Live Writer, or don't even know what that is, make sure to check this box.

- Core Update—Limits the access of core WordPress updates to Administrators only.

- Plugin Update—Removes plugin update notifications from all users who are not Administrators.

- Theme Update—Removes theme update information from non-administrators.

- WP Scanner — WordPress scanner is a free service that provides additional security details about your WordPress blog. You can learn more about this service at `http://blogsecurity.net/wpscan`.

- Block bad queries — Stops malicious URLs from being processed by WordPress.

Akismet

By Automattic (`http://automattic.com/`)

- **Why it's awesome**: Virtually eliminates spam on blog comments
- **Why it was picked**: Popularity and accuracy

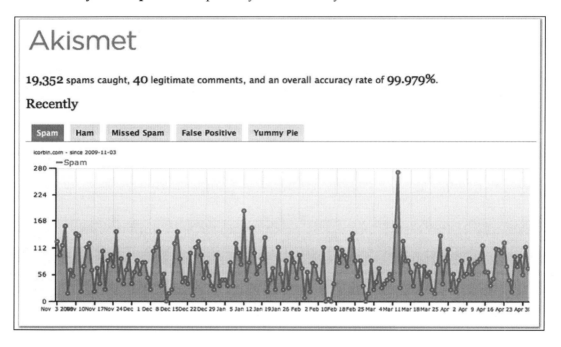

- **Manual Install URL**: `http://WordPress.org/extend/plugins/akismet/`
- **Automatic Install search term**: Akismet
- **Geek level**: Webmaster
- **Configuration location**: **Settings | Secure WP**
- **Used in**: Administrator

With WordPress, there is one thing you can always guarantee—lots of fake comments submitted by bots. Spam bots are nasty little programs that scour the web hunting for WordPress blogs to automatically submit comments to. Why do they do this? Because spamming comments is a really easy way to spread a website's URL to other websites.

Akismet, pronounced Ah-kiz-met, is a service provided by the original team who created WordPress-Automattic. This service scans each comment against a growing database of known spammers as well as evaluates the content of the comment for patterns that resemble spam.

In order to leverage this awesome plugin, you will need to have an Akismet API key. You can get a free API key (for non-commercial purposes) at `http://akismet.com/personal`.

 If you're a business and plan on making money through your blog, you can get a commercial key at `http://akismet.com/commercial`.

Historical Stats

	Spam detected	Ham detected	Missed spam	False positives
2010-05	183	0	0	0
2010-04	2,157	1	0	0
2010-03	1,945	8	0	0
2010-02	1,698	10	1	0
2010-01	2,263	0	0	0
2009-12	2,119	0	0	0
2009-11	2,430	0	2	0
2009-10	1,395	0	0	0
2009-09	1,846	0	0	0
2009-08	1,771	16	0	0
2009-07	637	1	0	0
2009-06	128	4	0	0
2009-05	196	0	1	0
2009-04	584	0	0	0

The preceding screenshot is of Akismet's historical spam for my personal blog iCorbin.com. The numbers are broken down into four categories: **Spam**, **Ham**, **Missed Spam**, and **False Positives**. Spam is a completely unsolicited comment, usually with a fake e-mail address. Ham is a comment that has a valid e-mail address, but questionable content. Missed spam is spam that Akismet happened to miss. False positives are comments that Akismet thought were spam but, in fact, were valid comments.

The number of spam messages caught in December 2009 hit 2,119, and this was on a blog that is far from popular and only attracts around 5,000 unique visitors a month.

Bad Behavior

By Bad Behavior Crew (http://www.bad-behavior.ioerror.us/)

- **Why it's awesome**: Unique way of stopping spammers before they get to your website
- **Why it was picked**: Easy to install with a high spam detection accuracy

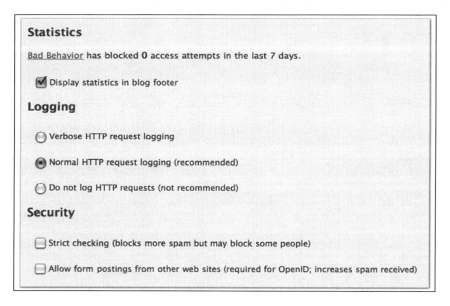

- **Manual Install URL**:
  http://WordPress.org/extend/plugins/bad-behavior
- **Automatic Install search term**: Bad Behavior
- **Geek level**: Newbie

- **Configuration location**: Tools | Bad Behavior
- **Used in**: Comments

Bad Behavior is a completely different way of keeping your blog spam-free. Unlike Akismet, Bad Behavior stops the spammer before they ever have a chance to submit a spam comment.

Bad Behavior does its magic by automatically blocking known spam bots from ever seeing your website by analyzing the delivery method that was used to hit your website. Once you have installed and activated the plugin, you're done and no additional configurations are needed.

While no spam silver bullet exists, using Bad Behavior in conjunction with Akismet will help ensure that your blog remains spam-free.

 A word of warning: Under certain circumstances, this plugin might falsely identify some users as bots, ultimately blocking them from ever seeing your website.

Upload+

By Pixline (http://pixline.net/)

- **Why it's awesome**: Set it and forget it
- **Why it was picked**: Automatically fixes uploaded filenames

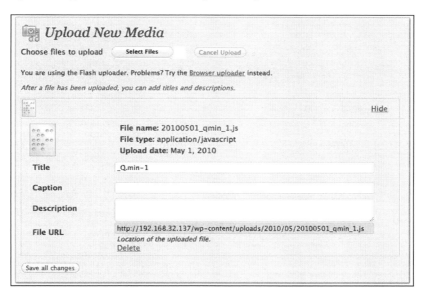

- **Manual Install URL**: `http://WordPress.org/extend/plugins/` `uploadplus/`
- **Automatic Install search term**: Upload+
- **Geek level**: Newbie
- **Configuration location**: No configuration required
- **Used in**: File uploads

If you're uploading a lot of media to your blog, or better yet, you have a bunch of non-technical people uploading pictures, files, and videos, then this plugin is a must have. It requires zero configuration and will automatically rename those crazy filenames non-technical people like to give their files to something more understandable. For example, it would convert "Suzy's big 16 Birthday Pics #2.jpg" to "suzys-big-16-birthday-pics-2.jpg".

WP Security Scan

By Michael Torbert (`http://semperfiwebdesign.com/`)

- **Why it's awesome**: It's more helpful than awesome, and a quick way of adding another layer of defense to your blog

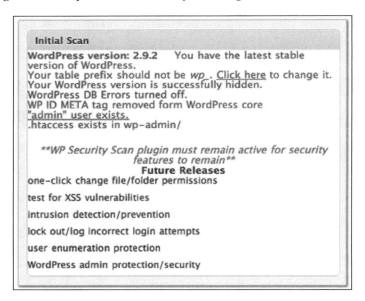

- **Manual Install URL**:
`http://WordPress.org/extend/plugins/wp-security-scan/`

- **Automatic Install search term**: WP Security Scan
- **Geek level**: Newbie
- **Configuration location**: Top Navigation | Security
- **Used in**: Administrator

WP Security Scan helps you to identify a few points of weaknesses that your blog might have with instructions on how to resolve these weakness. In order to see how your website fares, after installing and activating this plugin, head over to **Top Navigation | Security** from within your Administrator dashboard. Here you will see the items that WP Security Scan covers, including the following ones.

Latest version

WP Security Scan checks to see if you have the latest WordPress update installed. Not updating WordPress is the biggest security threat that exists, as the majority of updates fix software exploits that were discovered in previous versions. Running an outdated version of WordPress is like just asking to be hacked.

Table prefix

According to WP Security Scan, your database table prefix should not be the default wp_ and should report the results accordingly. WP Security Scan then gives you the option to rename your database tables to something other than wp_TABLENAME.

WARNING: I have had some issues while using the **Change your Table Prefix** feature of this plugin. After trying to use this feature, I was completely locked out of my WordPress blog and Administrator. You should avoid this feature unless you really know what you're doing.

Hiding Version # and Meta Tag ID

WordPress, by default, reports which version of WordPress your blog is running in the code of your site. The version number can be used by hackers to determine if you're running a version you compromised on. Hiding this field will help mask and deter hackers from trying to hack your site.

WordPress DB Errors

Errors are a fact of technical life; PHP and WordPress are no exception, and often PHP will display those errors to the user. This error information can be very valuable to hackers. Disabling these error messages will make hacking your site harder.

.htaccess in Admin folder

Ensuring that your wp-admin folder is not able to be browsed is absolutely key to the security of your blog. .htaccess files are super powerful configuration files on your website that can be used for many things, including rewriting URLs, redirecting users, and turning off whether your website lists a directories files to your visitors.

WP-DBManager

By Lester "GaMerZ" Chan (http://lesterchan.net/)

- **Why it's awesome**: Quick access to your blog's database
- **Why it was picked**: Ability to run SQL Queries without phpMyAdmin

- **Manual Install URL**:
  http://WordPress.org/extend/plugins/wp-dbmanager/
- **Automatic Install search term**: WP DBManager
- **Geek level**: WP Ninja
- **Configuration location: Top Navigation | Database**
- **Used in**: Comments

Having a healthy database is instrumental in having a blog that's fast and stable. However, unless you're a database administrator, database optimization is often over-looked. With **WP DBManager**, optimizing, repairing, and restoring your database is a snap.

Understanding your database's health

If you're a database administrator, feel free to skip this page. For the rest of us though, it's important to have a basic understanding of databases and, specifically, how your WordPress's life depends on it.

What is a database?

At the highest level, a database is only a set of files that can be read and written to by an application on the computer that runs your website. In the case of WordPress, the application is called MySQL and the files are called **databases**.

What is MySQL?

MySQL is one of the most popular open source database applications available. It's fast, it's free, and there are tons of documentation and conversations happening all over the web. To learn more about MySQL, visit `http://dev.mysql.com/`.

How does WordPress use MySQL?

WordPress stores all of the information for posts, pages, users, comments (and virtually everything else) in a MySQL database. Needless to say, over time, your database can become a rather large amount of information. While MySQL is phenomenal at sifting through and returning the right data really quickly, it also has a tendency to get messy, cluttered, and a little under the weather.

Repair, Optimize, and Backup

Database fatigue can cause all sorts of problems with WordPress, the worst being "Database not found". The more common problem is that the database is running slow or certain tables of data couldn't be found.

Repair—Databases that are written to and read from frequently do some very interesting things to make the response times incredibly fast. However, in achieving this speed, sometimes data gets out of place, erased, or corrupted. **Repair** is the terminology for when MySQL goes through the table and straightens things out.

Optimize—**Optimizing** your database is like a super repair; not only does it straighten things up but it also finds the most optimal locations for the data.

Backup—MySQL makes it very easy to export the data that exists in its databases. These **backups** can then be used to completely restore a past database or clone a new one (plus much, much more).

WP-DB-Backup

By Austin Matzko (`http://ilfilosofo.com/`)

- **Why it's awesome**: Makes backing up your blog's core database a breeze
- **Why it was picked**: Easy to use backup

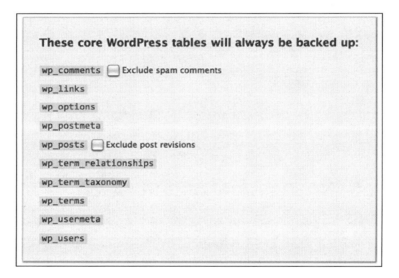

- **Manual Install URL**:
  `http://WordPress.org/extend/plugins/wp-db-backup/`
- **Automatic Install search term**: WP DB Backup
- **Geek level**: Newbie
- **Configuration location**: **Tools | Backup**
- **Used in**: Administrator

WP-DB-Backup makes automatically backing up your blog's database a snap. However, keep in mind that this only backs up your database content, not all of the images, plugins, and themes that your blog has installed. For those more advanced features, check out the next plugin.

WordPress Backup

By Austin Matzko (http://ilfilosofo.com/)

- **Why it's awesome**: Flexible backup of plugins, themes, and uploads

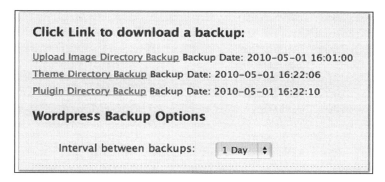

- **Manual Install URL**:
  http://WordPress.org/extend/plugins/WordPress-backup/
- **Automatic Install search term**: WordPress Backup
- **Geek level**: Webmaster
- **Configuration location**: **Settings | WordPress Backup**
- **Used in**: Administrator

Unlike the previous backup plugin WP-DB-Backup, **WordPress Backup** will also back up all of your blog's media content as well as the database content.

Maintenance Mode

By Michael Wohrer (http://sw-guide.de/)

- **Why it's awesome**: Quick and easy way to turn off access to your blog, except for your blog administrators

Maintenance Mode

Listy.me Store is currently undergoing scheduled maintenance.
Please try back **in 60 minutes**.

Sorry for the inconvenience.

- **Manual Install URL**:
  http://WordPress.org/extend/plugins/maintenance-mode/
- **Automatic Install search term**: Maintenance Mode
- **Geek level**: Newbie
- **Configuration location**: Settings | Maintenance Mode
- **Used in**: Site-wide

At some point in your WordPress career, you'll need to take your website down for maintenance. **Maintenance Mode** makes the experience of down time a little less annoying for the user. Once enabled, all users (minus administrators) will be shown a pretty little "Maintenance Mode" notice that can be 100 percent customized.

Customizing the maintenance notice

The default notice is good enough for most personal blogs. However, if you want to spice things up, visit **Settings | Maintenance Mode**.

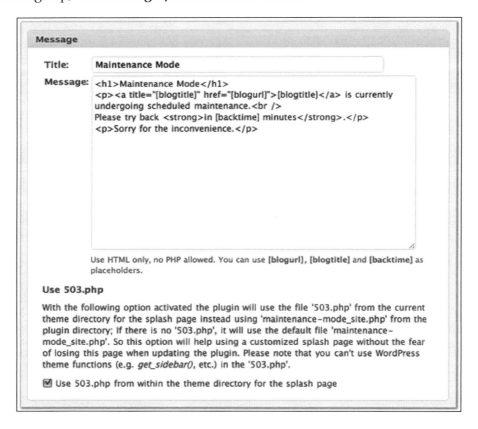

The message text field supports both HTML and CSS. You can also include [blogurl], [blogtitle], and [backtime]; each will be replaced with the actual information when a user visits the site.

WP-Optimize

By Ruhani Rabin (http://www.ruhanirabin.com/)

- **Why it's awesome**: Database optimization in one click

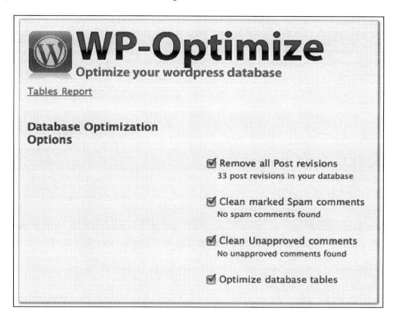

- **Manual Install URL**:
  http://WordPress.org/extend/plugins/wp-optimize/
- **Automatic Install search term**: WP Optimize
- **Geek level**: Newbie
- **Configuration location: Dashboard | WP Optimize**
- **Used in**: Database

Ruhani Rabin's simply brilliant plugin will help you keep your database optimized and pruned with virtually no work on your part. Not only does **WP-Optimize** keep your database optimized, but it also keeps your database lean and mean by deleting all unapproved comments and spam comments.

Quick Cache

By Primo Themes (http://www.primothemes.com/)

- **Why it's awesome**: The easiest and fastest way to improve your blog's speed
- **Why it was picked**: Out of the box setup is almost perfect

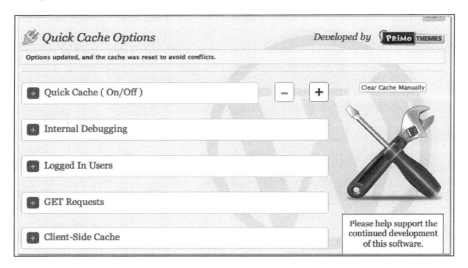

- **Manual Install URL**:
  http://WordPress.org/extend/plugins/quick-cache/
- **Automatic Install search term**: Quick Cache
- **Geek level**: Webmaster
- **Configuration location: Top Navigation | Quick Cache**
- **Used in**: Site-wide

Quick Cache is one of the newest caching plugins available for WordPress, and if I do say so myself, it is awesome! Unlike the other caching systems, Quick Cache requires absolutely no configuration, and in my experience, it "just works". You'll be blown away at how this easy plugin turns your website into a screaming speed demon.

Quick Cache Options explained

While Quick Cache requires no additional setup, it offers a slew of configuration options.

- **Quick Cache ON/OFF** — Enable or disable caching by selecting enabled or disabled from the drop-down box.

- **Internal Debugging** — As of this writing, **Internal Debugging** should be left alone and is mainly reserved for future development.

- **Logged In Users** — In some cases, you might not want to cache pages for logged in users. Since most traffic to your website is from non-logged in users, it's safe to leave this feature set to "True". However, if you have a ton of members, then you might need to consider setting this feature to "False".

- **Get Request** — If you're using WordPress's SEO Friendly Links, for example: `myblog.com/2010/04/04/mypost-name` as opposed to `myblog.com/?postid=123`, then leave this option set to "True". However, if you're using the latter or "ugly" URLs, set this feature to "False".

- **Client-Side Cache** — If you change your website content, CSS, or images frequently, it's recommended that you leave this option set to "False". Otherwise, if set to "True", website-visitors/browsers will store (remember) your JavaScript, CSS, and image files for quite a long time.

- **Cache Expiration Time** — This setting allows you to define how long the content and pages should be cached for. The default value, 3600 seconds, would be fine for most websites but feel free to tweak it according to your taste.

- **Dynamic Cache Pruning** — If you want your new posts to show up instantly — both as a post and on the home page, it's recommended to select the **Single + Front Page** option. When selected, any time a new page or post is added, the previously cached version is pruned and replaced with the new content.

- **No-Cache URL Patterns** — You can set specific URL patterns that, if matched, will not be cached.

- **No-Cache Referrer Patterns** — Configure caching based on where a user originated.

- **No-Cache User-Agent Patterns** — Configure specific types of browsers and bots to never see cached content.

- **Mutex File Locking**—File locking is a technical process that is used when WordPress is reading or writing files. Quick Cache offers two different methods for file locking. It's recommended that unless you are hosting your blog with a cloud hosting provider that you use **Semaphore**. For those on Cloud Hosting services like Rack Space Cloud, it's recommended that you use **Flock**.

- **MD5 Version Salt**—For advanced users only! Use this option to create a custom hash for the name of the cached files.

Error Reporting

By Mittineague (`http://www.mittineague.com/`)

- **Why it's awesome**: Errors are not awesome, but knowing when they're happening is

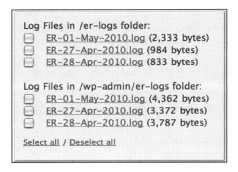

- **Manual Install URL**: `http://WordPress.org/extend/plugins/error-reporting/`

- **Automatic Install search term**: Error Reporting

- **Geek level**: WP Ninja

- **Configuration location: Settings | ErrorReporting**

- **Used in**: Administrator

Error Reporting allows you to know when different types of errors happen on your website. With its highly customizable settings, you can be notified when anything gets squirrelly with your blog, including standard WordPress errors, plugin errors, and even theme errors.

Auto Delete old log files

Unattended log files have a tendency to grow out of control and consume vast amounts of computer space. **Auto Delete** will automatically delete log files older than a week or a month, depending on how you set up your configuration.

Configuration

- **Log Errors?** — Turn the entire plugin on or off
- **Include All Error Types?** — To report on all errors or not
- **Error Types** — The types of errors that should be logged
- **Include All Folders?** — Select which folders should be monitored for errors, including wp-admin, wp-content, plugins, and wp-includes
- **Folders** — Available folders to monitor for errors
- **Log Repeat Errors?** — Limiting the number of times a specific error is logged will help limit the log file-size

Summary

In this chapter, we covered many ways to help secure your blog. It's very important to remember that no single action can protect your blog completely. But with a few simple plugins and a routine of backing up, you should be ok, no matter what happens to your site.

- Limit Login Attempts — Quickly stop "brute force" login hacking
- Secure WordPress — Deactivate some of WordPress's default elements that cause security issues
- Akismet — Cut comment spam to almost nothing
- Bad Behavior — Stop spam bots and hackers before they ever get to your site
- Upload+ — Ensure all files uploaded to your blog are properly named
- WP Security Scan — Scan for weaknesses in your blogs security
- WP-DBManager — Quickly run queries and optimize and repair your WordPress database
- WP-DB-Backup — A simple-to-use database backup plugin
- WordPress Backup — A comprehensive backup solution for all of your blog's content

- Maintenance Mode—Display a nice customized message while your site is down for repairs.
- WP-Optimizer—Quickly repair and prune your WordPress database.
- Quick Cache—Super simple site-wide caching.
- Error Reporting—Be notified when specific errors occur on your blog.

In the next chapter, we will cover a handful of plugins for the power administrator—plugins that really pump up the vanilla WordPress administrator section.

9
Power Admin

Since you're reading this book, it's fair to say that you spend more time in the WordPress admin area than you do at the frontend of your blog. While most plugins in this book are focused on a blog's frontend, this chapter will cover great plugins to make your WordPress administer a productive powerhouse.

In this chapter we will cover:

- Making your WordPress administration beautiful and usable
- Keeping track of visitors' activities
- Accessing links to your admin from your blog's frontend
- Making plugin and theme editing a snap with a real code editor
- Adding additional links to third-party services
- Checking if all links on your blog are valid
- Sending mass e-mails to users and groups
- Adding powerful CMS-like features
- Customizing your blog's appearance, based on specific conditions

Fluency Admin

By Dean Robinson (http://deanjrobinson.com/)

- **Why it's awesome**: Straight up—it turns your boring WordPress administrator into a beautiful, keyboard-friendly, and highly usable content manager

- **Why it was picked**: No other admin theme pays attention to the details that Fluency does

- **Manual Install URL**: http://wordpress.org/extend/plugins/fluency-admin/
- **Automatic Install search term**: Fluency Admin
- **Geek level**: Newbie
- **Configuration location**: **Settings | Fluency Settings**
- **Used in**: All Admin

Once you have installed **Fluency Admin**, your view of the WordPress's administrator will change forever. Yes that's a bold statement, but once you have experienced the quick key access, the sexy black gloss and the attention to detail that Dean paid—the out of the box WordPress admin will feel, well, ancient.

Quick key access

Not only does Fluency Admin make the administrator look good, but it also helps you become significantly more productive, navigating all of your blog's administrative options. Hands-down, the coolest feature of this plugin is the ability to use simple key strokes to activate different sections of the WordPress administrator.

Take the last screenshot as an example. Each menu item has a letter or a number to the right of its label. In this case, you would need to type **P** to activate the **Posts** menu. Then you can type **2** to automatically select the **Add New** post action. Once you have used this feature a few times, you'll find that you're navigating your blog's admin at almost the speed of light.

Styling the login screen

Another killer feature that Fluency Admin offers, but for some reason is disabled by default, is its option to restyle the boring default **WordPress Login Page**.

To enable this feature, visit **Settings | Fluency Admin** and select the checkbox next to **Fluency Login Style**.

StatPress

By Daniele Lippi (`http://www.irisco.it/`)

- **Why it's awesome**: StatPress gives you detailed insights into what's happening on your blog in real time
- **Why it was picked**: Ease of install, stability, owning the stats versus renting the stats with a third party

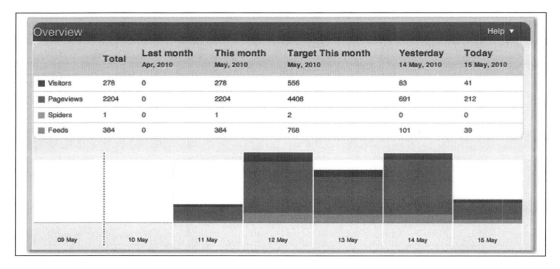

- **Manual Install URL**: `http://wordpress.org/extend/plugins/statpress/`
- **Automatic Install search term**: StatPress
- **Geek level**: Newbie
- **Configuration location**: **Top Navigation | StatPress | Options**
- **Used in**: Administration

Statistics are key to understanding what's working on your website and what's not. **StatPress** gives you all of the same basic information that a third-party service like Google Analytics does. However, with StatPress, you actually own the data versus merely renting it. Also, most third-party analytic tools use JavaScript to track visitor movement. This additional JavaScript call increases the load time of your website and misses any visitors who do not have JavaScript enabled.

Key datapoints

StatPress collects a lot of data, and it's recommended you spend some serious time getting to know each report and how to use its analysis to continually improve your blog. However, to start out, here are the top five reports that you should definitely be paying attention to.

Latest Referrers

One of the keys to growing your blog is to know how people are finding it. With the **Latest Referrers** report, you will see a continual stream of external websites that are sending you visitors. Try to find the patterns in this data. Once you figure out which links are sending the most traffic, you can start to nurture the relationship with those sites in hopes to get additional write-ups, comments, and ultimately more visitors.

Last referrers

Date	Time	URL	Result
May 23, 2010	15:05:09	http://pipes.yahoo.com/pipes/pipe.info?_id=4920ce102a29e829a98b0deb107d7680	page viewed
May 23, 2010	15:05:08	http://pipes.yahoo.com/pipes/pipe.info?_id=4920ce102a29e829a98b0deb107d7680	page viewed
May 23, 2010	14:23:31	http://www.omg-facts.com/page/18	page viewed
May 23, 2010	14:11:03	http://pipes.yahoo.com/pipes/pipe.info?_id=2a441b0dfbac035a917c891a8a8c2678	page viewed
May 23, 2010	13:57:32	http://pipes.yahoo.com/pipes/pipe.info?_id=2a441b0dfbac035a917c891a8a8c2678	page viewed
May 23, 2010	13:57:32	http://pipes.yahoo.com/pipes/pipe.info?_id=2a441b0dfbac035a917c891a8a8c2678	page viewed
May 23, 2010	13:10:41	http://pipes.yahoo.com/pipes/pipe.info?_id=2a441b0dfbac035a917c891a8a8c2678	page viewed
May 23, 2010	13:09:53	http://pipes.yahoo.com/pipes/pipe.info?_id=2a441b0dfbac035a917c891a8a8c2678	page viewed
May 23, 2010	13:01:41	http://pipes.yahoo.com/pipes/pipe.info?_id=4920ce102a29e829a98b0deb107d7680	page viewed
May 23, 2010	13:01:40	http://pipes.yahoo.com/pipes/pipe.info?_id=4920ce102a29e829a98b0deb107d7680	page viewed

Search Terms

You absolutely have to know what keywords are being used to find your website. These keywords are what Google and the other search engines think your blog is about. With this knowledge, you can start blogging about similar content, strategically dropping in those keywords in your posts. Doing this will create a feedback loop to the search engine bots and ultimately increase your site's overall rank.

Last search terms

Date	Time	Terms	Engine	Result
May 23, 2010	13:17:45	india has more honors studentsd	Google	page viewed
May 23, 2010	13:11:57	mashups music wrangler	Google	page viewed
May 23, 2010	13:11:14	mashups music wrangler	Google	page viewed
May 23, 2010	10:14:14	linkedin public profile php	Google	page viewed
May 23, 2010	01:00:03	mac mini vs	Google	page viewed
May 23, 2010	00:42:30	theme wordpress linkedin	Google	page viewed
May 22, 2010	21:45:48	compare mac mini and acer	Google	page viewed
May 22, 2010	17:41:09	ecommerce buttons	Google	page viewed
May 22, 2010	16:53:27	mac mini or acer revo	Google	page viewed
May 22, 2010	16:44:46	how to send anonymous tweet	Google	page viewed

Operating Systems

Knowing which operating system your visitors use is helpful if people are consuming your blog with non-PC devices. For example, if you have a ton of traffic from the iPhone or Android, you should consider making your blog mobile-friendly.

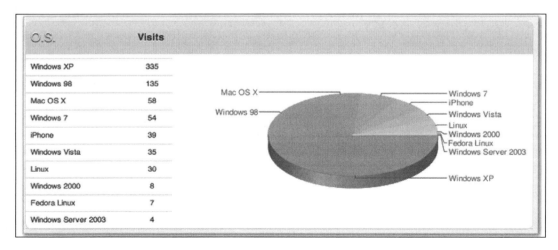

O.S.	Visits
Windows XP	335
Windows 98	135
Mac OS X	58
Windows 7	54
iPhone	39
Windows Vista	35
Linux	30
Windows 2000	8
Fedora Linux	7
Windows Server 2003	4

Browsers Used

Browser traffic helps you understand how technically savvy your users are. If, for example, you have very little Internet Explorer traffic, you could start leveraging more HTML 5 and CSS 3 syntax to make your blog sing. On the opposite side, if you have a ton of Internet Explorer traffic, then you might need to spend more time making your site look perfect in IE.

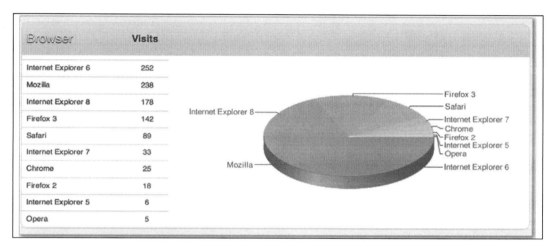

Spy View

One of most instantly gratifying features of StatPress is the **Spy View**. **Spy View** allows you to see what's happening on your website right now. Not only does it show you where people are coming from, but it also helps you see that people are actually reading your stuff. This emotional stoking will significantly boost your blogging motivation.

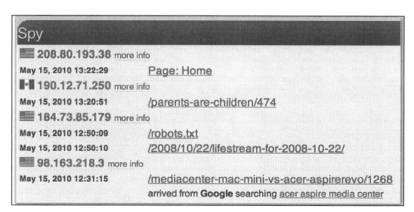

404 Notifier

By Alex King (http://alexking.org/)

- **Why it's awesome**: Turns visitors into 404 hunters and notifies you instantly if they find anything

- **Why it was picked**: Simplicity; Alex King rocks at WordPress plugins

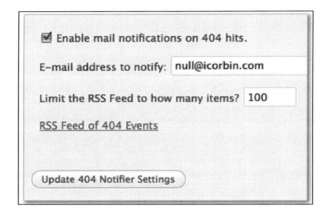

- **Manual Install URL**: http://wordpress.org/extend/plugins/404-notifier/

- **Automatic Install search term**: 404 Notifier

- **Geek level**: Newbie

- **Configuration location**: **Settings | 404 Notifier**

- **Used in**: Administrator

If you've been running a blog for a long time, there's a good chance that many of the links you referenced in the past are no longer valid. Sure, you could manually go through all of your posts and hunt down each of these missing pages, but where's the fun in that? Instead, use **404 Notifier** and let your blog's traffic find all of the broken links for you. Once a visitor hits a page that no longer exists, an e-mail will automatically be fired off to an e-mail address that you provide. Additionally, you can subscribe to the 404 Feed and track any missing pages through your favorite RSS reader.

Shockingly Big IE6 Warning

By Matias S (http://www.incerteza.org/blog/)

- **Why it's awesome**: Because Internet Explorer 6 is awful, and this plugin will make sure that everyone who visits your site with IE6 knows it

- **Manual Install URL**: http://wordpress.org/extend/plugins/ shockingly-big-ie6-warning/
- **Automatic Install search term**: Shockingly Big IE6 Warning
- **Geek level**: Newbie
- **Configuration location**: **Settings | S. Big IE6 Warning**
- **Used In**: All pages

Internet Explorer 6 was hands down the best browser when it came out in 2001. However, its success has now become its greatest weakness. Because of its worldwide adoption, it became very attractive to hackers, and over the years, countless exploits have been discovered and leveraged to infect people's computers. To this day, IE6 has a 20 percent market share—developers and designers globally shriek at this truth, as IE6 is one of the hardest browsers to design on.

Shockingly Big IE6 Warning will only warn IE6 users one time; after that, they will never be presented with the message again. While Shockingly Big, by default, does show, a well a shockingly big warning, you can also customize it to display a smaller message at the top of the browser window.

Admin Links Widget

By Keith Murray (`http://kdmurray.net/`)

- **Why it's awesome**: Admin Links Widget lets you quickly access specific pages inside of the administrator from anywhere on your blog
- **Why it was picked**: Easy to set up, ability to pick which admin links are displayed

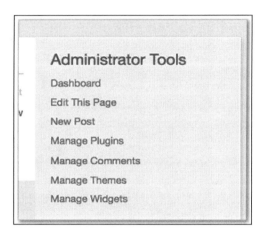

- **Manual Install URL**: `http://wordpress.org/extend/plugins/admin-links-sidebar-widget/`
- **Automatic Install search term**: Admin Links Sidebar Widget
- **Geek level**: Newbie
- **Configuration location**: None
- **Used in**: All pages

Most themes don't offer direct links to the blog's administrator. This lack of access requires you to manually visit the administration area by typing it in the browser. This time sucking action is no longer a problem thanks to the **Admin Links Widget**. Admin Links Widget, so properly named, is a widget that can be added to your blog that lists out commonly used administrative links. This widget will only be displayed to the users who are logged in as an administrator.

WordPress Admin Bar

By Viper007Bond (`http://viper007bond.com/`)

- **Why it's awesome**: Quickly access every part of your WordPress administrator from anywhere on your website
- **Why it was picked**: Easy to set up, access to every admin link

- **Manual Install URL**: `http://wordpress.org/extend/plugins/wordpress-admin-bar/`
- **Automatic Install search term**: WordPress Admin Bar
- **Geek level**: Newbie
- **Configuration location**: None
- **Used In**: All pages

Unlike the previous plugin, **WordPress Admin Bar** will display every link available in your administrator in a clean, easy-to-access bar at the top of your website, if you're logged in.

Code Editor

By Naden Badalgogtapeh (blog)

- **Why it's awesome**: Desktop-like code editing from within WordPress!
- **Why it was picked**: Line numbers, tabbing, and many languages are supported

- **Manual Install URL**:
  http://wordpress.org/extend/plugins/code-editor/
- **Automatic Install search term**: Code Editor
- **Geek level**: Webmaster
- **Used in**: Theme editor, plugin editor

The out-of-the-box plugin and theme editor provided by WordPress is simply a gigantic textbox. Thus, trying to edit HTML, CSS, JavaScript, and PHP in a traditional text field is pretty frustrating since it lacks the ability to handle the use of tabs. **Code Editor** will create an almost desktop-like code editor right in your browser, with code coloring, text indentions, and line numbers.

WordPress Admin QuickMenu

By Christopher Ross (`http://www.thisismyurl.com/`)

- **Why it's awesome**: Instant, clickable action to any of the online tools you frequently use

- **Manual Install URL**:
  `http://wordpress.org/extend/plugins/wordpress-admin-quickmenu/`
- **Automatic Install search term**: WordPress Admin QuickMenu
- **Geek level**: Webmaster
- **Configuration location**: **Top Navigation | Quick Menus**
- **Used in**: Administrator

WordPress Admin QuickMenu makes your most commonly used third party services just a click away. For example, you might want to link directly to Google Analytics, your online e-mail account, or any of those blogs you follow for inspiration.

Setting up your links

1. Visit **Quick Menu | Quick Menu**.

2. For each line, add a **Title**, the **URL (hyperlink)**, and select which level of user can see this link (security).

3. Click on **Save Changes**.

4. Click on the **Reload** link.

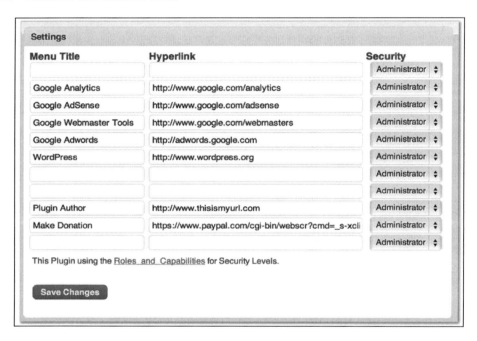

Email Users

By Vincent Prat (http://www.vincentprat.info/)

- **Why it's awesome**: Ability to target e-mails to different segments of your community in a very simple package

- **Why it was picked**: No setup required, fast installation, popular download

- **Manual Install URL**: http://wordpress.org/extend/plugins/email-users/
- **Automatic Install search term**: Email Users
- **Geek level**: Webmaster
- **Configuration location: Top Navigation | Email**
- **Used In**: Administrator

You might be asking yourself, why do I want to e-mail my users? I have RSS feeds, tweets, Facebook updates, and just about every other means of communicating with my readers. The answer is actually simple: e-mail converts. Even in this time of spam overload, e-mails convert significantly higher than social media updates and Google AdWords. If you have a reader base, then you have one of the most valuable assets online—users' e-mail addresses and their attention.

E-mail ideas

With **Email Users,** you now have the ability to send your messages directly to your users' e-mail addresses. So what do you say? Here are a few ideas that you can leverage to increase your readership and build a lasting brand online.

Exclusive e-mailer

People love to feel special, especially if they think all of the other people-in-the-know are doing it. Just look at the long lines outside select New York clubs. Create a weekly or monthly e-mail that covers topics that you don't specifically talk about on your blog. However, do talk about the exclusive newsletter and its general contents in as many spots as possible. This will help motivate the non-registered readers to sign up for your blog simply to get the e-mail.

Special deals and offers

Give your readers access to special deals and promotions. Don't have any special deals? Find a business in your market and ask if you could have a discount code to provide your readers; you'd be amazed at what companies will give you for zero-cost marketing.

Helping a cause

People are apt to react when they feel they are contributing to a good cause. Leverage your valuable e-mail addresses to help promote whatever your cause may be.

Tips and tricks

If you're running a blog that focuses on creating things, such as design, development, and so on, create an exclusive newsletter that includes tips and ideas that are only available by e-mail.

Broken Link Checker

By Janis Elsts (`http://w-shadow.com/blog/`)

- **Why it's awesome**: It checks for any broken links throughout your entire site
- **Why it was picked**: Simple interface, checks external links too!

- **Manual Install URL**: `http://wordpress.org/extend/plugins/broken-link-checker/`
- **Automatic Install search term**: Broken Link Checker
- **Geek level**: Webmaster
- **Configuration location: Tools | Broken Links**
- **Used in**: Administrator

404 is a code name for a missing page or a webpage that no longer exists. Over the years, I am sure you have linked to tons of websites that are either dead in the water or have changed their website's URL structure. **Broken Link Checker** will try to go through all of your previous posts and find any links to websites that are no longer reachable. Along with the 404 Notify plugin mentioned earlier in this chapter, you will never have another missing page or link within your blog. Unlike 404 Notify, Broken Link Checker covers external websites as well as internal pages.

Admin Management Xtended

By Oliver Schlobe (`http://www.schloebe.de/`)

- **Why it's awesome**: It makes managing pages and posts significantly faster and more efficient

- **Manual Install URL**: http://wordpress.org/extend/plugins/admin-management-xtended/
- **Automatic Install search term**: Admin Management Xtended
- **Geek level**: Webmaster
- **Configuration location**: None
- **Used in**: Administrator

Admin Management Xtended adds a handful of additional Content Management System-like features to your posts and pages management screen. These features allow you to quickly edit, delete, comment, rearrange, and show/hide content. All of these actions happen using AJAX, so you no longer will need to wait for the page to reload after making a modification to a post or a page.

Understanding the interface

Admin Management Xtended will add a few more icons to your posts and pages management screen. Here is a breakdown of each new icon and how it will affect your posts:

- Title Pencil icon—quickly changes the title of a post or a page
- Author Pencil icon—quickly changes the author of a page or a post
- Action Checkbox—toggles if a post or a page is active or inactive
- Calendar Icon—changes the publication date of a post or a page
- Paperclip Icon—changes the URL slug of a post or a page
- Comment Bubble Icon—toggles if comments are on or off

Menu Manager

By Sulaeman (`http://www.feelinc.me/`)

- **Why it's awesome**: Tons of control over how WordPress displays your menu navigation
- **Why it was picked**: Flexible layout model, recently updated, community loved

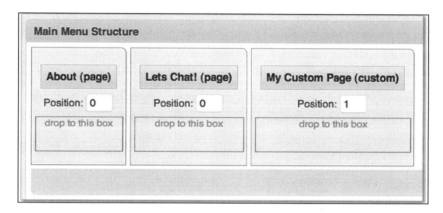

- **Manual Install URL**: `http://wordpress.org/extend/plugins/menu-manager/`
- **Automatic Install search term**: Menu Manager
- **Geek level**: Webmaster
- **Configuration location: Settings | Menu Manager**
- **Used in**: Administrator

WordPress' navigation system leaves a little to be desired. Specifically, controlling exactly how your blog's navigation is rendered. **Menu Manager** allows you to decide which pages are to be displayed, which pages should be submenus, and the ability to add custom items that point to any URL.

Simple Tags

By Amaury Balmer (`http://www.herewithme.fr/`)

- **Why it's awesome**: Easiest way to organize all of your blog posts' tags
- **Why it was picked**: Integrations for auto tagging, ease of use

Post title	Terms : Post tags
Open letter to Steve Jobs. You broke my heart today.	apple, jobs
Send an anonymous Tweet to any Twitter User	listy, twitter
Reasons I like having kids.	kids, parenting
4 Amusing Twitter Users	listy, twitter
The Listy API – sorta	API, listy
Building a media center for less than 500 bucks	acer, mac, media center
5 Cool Usability folks to follow on Twitter	listy, twitter, Usability
3 web apps I'll swear by.	apps, listy, tech
Making Organic Ice Cream – a Listy Embed Test	food, listy, receipt
Listy.me idea vs. reality	apps, listy
UFC 533 Light Weight Champion of the World	family
New pet project Listy.me and a plea to my future self.	app, listy, remember
ChaCha API with PHP	API, chacha, PHP
3 awesome small business ecommerce options.	ecommerce, opensource, OSS, PHP
Free eCommerce Solutions Showdown.	ecommerce

- **Manual Install URL**:
  `http://wordpress.org/extend/plugins/simple-tags/`
- **Automatic Install search term**: Simple Tags
- **Geek level**: Webmaster
- **Configuration location**: **Settings | Simple Tags**
- **Used in**: Administrator

Simple Tags is a complete tag management solution for WordPress. Tags are simply a word that describes a chunk of content. For example, if you write a blog post covering the latest advances in gouda cheese, then the post tags might be cheese and gouda and breakthrough.

Simple Tag offers multiple methods for managing your tags, including:

- Batch tag renaming, deleting, and adding
- Post quick tagging
- Importing of tags
- Type-ahead tags
- Auto link tags in post content

Configuring third party Taxonomy Services

One of Simple Tags's awesome features is its integration with OpenCalais, Alchemy, and Zemanta. All three services focus on finding common tags within large amounts of text. From within the **Settings | Simple Tag,** click the **Administration** tab. The last three options are where you will need to provide an **API key** from each service. You can register for an API key for these services at:

- OpenCalais: `http://www.opencalais.com/`
- Alchemy: `http://www.alchemyapi.com/`
- Zemanta: `http://developer.zemanta.com/`

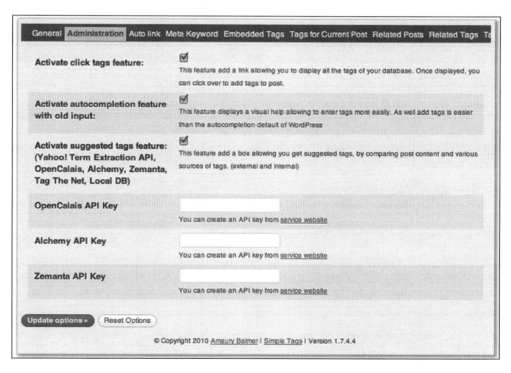

Once installed, your blog posts and pages will be scraped and analyzed by the Taxonomy Services and tags will be automatically recommended. The more services you connect to, the broader the suggestions will ultimately be.

Redirection

By John Godley (`http://urbangiraffe.com/`)

- **Why it's awesome**: Redirect users to the right spot even if you change your domain or permlink structures
- **Why it was picked**: Simple to install, regex support

- **Manual Install URL**: `http://wordpress.org/extend/plugins/redirection/`
- **Automatic Install search term**: Redirection
- **Geek level**: WP Ninja
- **Configuration location**: **Tools | Redirection**
- **Used in**: Administrator

When you move your blog, change your domain or change your permalink structure—all of those links indexed in Google, Yahoo, and MSN are no longer valid. This type of move, unless addressed, can cause your site to plummet in search engine traffic.

With John's **Redirection** plugin, you can now easily set up an unlimited number of redirects using the power of regular expressions, without ever having to touch your `.htaccess` file. In addition to changing your permalink structures, this plugin can also be used to catch and redirect normal 404 pages.

While the explanation of regular expressions is far beyond the scope of this book, you can start your research at the following sites:

- PHP sepecific regular expressions: `http://www.webcheatsheet.com/php/regular_expressions.php`

- Regex documentation: `http://www.regular-expressions.info/`
- Regex online tool: `http://www.gskinner.com/RegExr/`

Widget Logic
By Alan Trewartha (`http://freakytrigger.co.uk/author/alan/`)

- **Why it's awesome**: Target widgets to specific parts of your blog
- **Why it was picked**: Support for all WordPress conditional tags

- **Manual Install URL**: `http://wordpress.org/extend/plugins/widget-logic/`
- **Automatic Install search term**: Simple Tags
- **Geek level**: WP Ninja
- **Configuration location**: None
- **Used in**: Administrator

Really, most blogs only contain three different types of pages, namely, the home page, the post page, and the category page, hence the lack of a need to have different widgets on different pages. However, if you're building a full blown website (not just a blog) using WordPress, then the need to target specific widgets to a given page is most helpful. **Widget Logic** allows you to target specific pages and other conditions, that, when met, will display a specific widget.

Once installed, every widget you put on your blog's sidebar will now have a new field at the bottom called **WP Logic** — inside this text box is where you will include the logic that defines whether or not to display the widget. The logic that is available is basically any PHP function or standard WordPress Conditional Tag. You can see a full list of these tags at `http://codex.wordpress.org/Conditional_Tags`.

Commonly used logic

The logic that is commonly used is as follows:

- `is_home()` — your blog's home page
- `is_page('page-name')` — if the current page is
- `!is_page("exclude-from-this-page-name")` — show on every page but one listed
- `is_category(array(1,3,4,5))` — is a category with ID 1, 3, 4, or 5
- `is_single()` — is a single post page
- `is_category()` — is a category page

Summary

Considering how much time is spent in WordPress's back office, it's worth the time to make it as easy, effective, and pretty as possible. We should all shake the hand of every developer who spends time building these non-public facing plugins that make our lives so much easier.

- Fluency Admin — Making your WordPress administrator beautiful and usable
- StatPress — Tracking every step of a visitor's experience on your blog
- 404 Notifier — Keeping track of missing pages
- Shockingly Big IE6 Warning — Helping those who are internet-challenged
- Admin Links Widget — Quick access to select admin links from anywhere on your site
- WordPress Admin Bar — Quick access to every admin link from anywhere on your site
- Code Editor — Desktop-like code editing directly in your browser
- WordPress Admin QuickMenu — Quick access to external websites directly from your menu
- Broken Link Checker — Validates that all URLs on your website actually go somewhere
- Email Users — Send mass e-mails to users and groups
- Admin Management Xtended — Adds powerful CMS/Ajax features to your post and page management
- Menu Manager — Customizes how your blog's navigation is rendered
- Simple Tags — Manages all of your blog's tags quickly and efficiently
- Redirection — Controls redirects within your blog using the power of regular expressions
- Widget Logic — Customizes which widgets are to be displayed

10
Time for Action

People just like you are building million dollar empires built on WordPress. This is really worth repeating—**people just like you are making millions of dollars using WordPress**. Yes I know! That sounds like a campy infomercial line, but my dear readers, it's exceedingly true. Nevertheless, there is absolutely no reason why you can't be one of them or at least make enough money from WordPress that you can start to think about quitting your day-time job.

In this chapter, we'll quickly cover the following:

- Prototyping with WordPress
- How real business models can run on WordPress
- Making money selling themes, plugins, and digital goods
- Offering job boards, WordPress hosting, and corporate blogging software
- Additional resources to learn more about WordPress and WordPress Plugins

The open source business model

There's a lot of debate on the validity of building a flourishing business on top of open source technologies like WordPress. More often than not, this resilience is directly related to past ideals that are quickly becoming extinct. Thanks to open source technology, we, the people, can now compete on the same playing field as the biggest colossal companies in the world. Open source is empowerment.

Open source, if used properly, can also be insanely profitable. Take Google for example; practically all of the technology that powers Google is open source. Google also continually supports and releases code back to the community. Apple, the company that most view as "closed", heavily relies on open source code for almost all of its products. Safari, Apple's web browser, is based on the open source project "Webkit", which, ironically, is the same base project that Google uses for its own web browser, Chrome.

Open source matters big time — but it depends on how you use it. Don't expect to be able to make some software package and sell it for $10,000 — those days are quickly dying. Instead, use the technology to offer a better service, experience, or product.

WordPress for prototyping

WordPress is, in my humble opinion, the best platform to prototype your product on. Regardless if your final product will be powered by WordPress or not, the rapid development cycle makes its value unimaginable. Have an idea for an online business? In less than 36 hours, a hardworking weekend, you could have it built to 80 percent of what the final product could be. Prototyping is a 1000 times better than a business plan; a prototype shows that you're serious and have invested heavily into your product, even though 90 percent of it was built using code that already existed.

Building a prototype (or a business for that matter) on WordPress might seem a bit intimidating if you're not a developer or a designer who really understands the guts. However, this little paragraph is to calm those irrational fears. WordPress is simple for any developer who knows PHP. PHP developers are all over the place and many of them are looking for work. There's even a WordPress developer-specific job board that you can post your projects/gigs at `http://jobs.wordpress.net/`.

Real business models with WordPress

Of course there is an unlimited number of business models that could be built on WordPress or any other open source platform for that matter. However, this unlimited number is quite overwhelming if you don't already have an idea of what you want to build. In the next section, I will cover a handful of plausible business models that you could start building tomorrow — I can't promise you'll make millions; I can't even promise that you'll make $2, but I can promise that building your own business will be one of the most rewarding experiences you'll ever have.

Selling digital goods

There is no business finer than one that sells virtual goods. Unlimited inventory, not needing a warehouse and new products are just a few clicks and swipes of the mouse away. Selling digital goods is crazily profitable if you have the right goods.

Take `IconDock.com` as an example; they sell high quality icons for about a dollar an icon. Around 60,000 unique visitors come to IconDock each month, and best of all, they are powering it with WordPress and the plugin WP e-Commerce.

Know how to take photos? Sell royalty free photos. Know how to design icons? Sell icons. Know how to print T-Shirts? Sell T-Shirts and Illustrator files of T-Shirt designs for $2 bucks a download. Don't know how to design? Go to the next Designer Meetup in your town and start talking—find out which ones can learn how to design themes for WordPress, then become their best friend.

Mark my words, the Digital Goldmine is just starting and it's going to be huge. :Look at Facebook games like Farmville, or the online poker game Zynga that lets you buy more "tokens" with real money but offers no real money payback. It's brilliant—and all you need to do is find that idea, pull it out of your head, and starting selling.

Selling themes

As of this writing, there are 27,000 monthly Google searches for "Premium Wordpress Themes". That shows there are a lot of people who will buy high quality themes.

Like plugins, themes can be fairly easy to put together if you have the right people or skill sets. WooThemes (`http://woothemes.com`) has shown that you can build a million dollar business, almost without ever talking to a single customer by selling high quality WordPress themes.

Themes are a very popular commodity that can quickly generate lots of traffic to your website (the free theme especially). There are hundreds of websites that focus purely on showcasing free WordPress themes. Collectively, those sites and the websites using your free theme will increase your own website's overall search engine ranking.

You can even copy SmashingMagazines's approach and commission designers to create themes for your business—you ultimately pay them a flat rate for the full rights to the theme and then give the theme away for free. These free themes will be the light that attracts the customers—once you have them, you upsell premium themes priced anywhere between $5 and $40 per theme.

Take WooTheme as an example—every time they release a new free theme, it gets featured in every single "Top 10 free WordPress themes…" blog post and article that is covering the web—completely free marketing.

Selling plugins

50,000 unique visitors a month are browsing and buying from WPPlugins.com, who, at the time of writing, has almost no competition. The market place, à la App Store, for WordPress is a gargantuan untapped market. Developers can easily charge anywhere from $5 to $300 when selling a plugin on WPPlugins.

The market that WPPlugins currently occupies is waiting for a competitor to come along and offer service and support, as well as a built-in AppStore directly in WordPress.

Don't forget about our big corporations, who are turning to WordPress more and more for their own internal websites. These big corporations will pay big bucks for plugins that help connect their different systems.

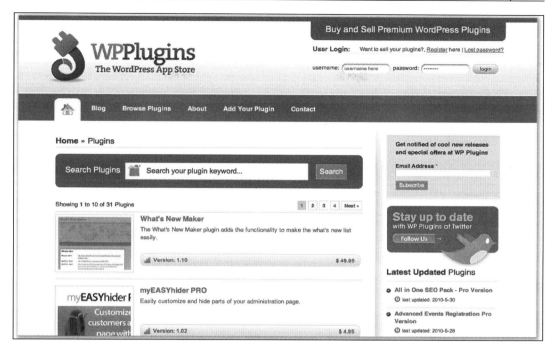

Selling advertising spots

The days of building the best tech blog or best gardening blog and dominating the market are virtually over. While sites like TechCrunch and Gizmodo make millions from advertising, they also have been building their brand and site content for a long time—competing with them would most definitely mean suicide. However, there's still the niche!

Picking a market niche (like Fender Guitars or Chemical-Free Gardening) can lead to a dedicated following of people who, like you, obsess about your passion. Once you have your niche site up and running, start calling the huge companies who are in the same general space.

Job board

WordPress, along with a few strategically installed plugins, can make one amazing social job board. For example, with the $97 premium plugin WPJobBoard (`http://wpjobboard.net/`), you can start charging anywhere between $20 to $300 per job posting, depending on visitor demographics and traffic.

The world desperately needs more niche job boards in the market, ones that are friendly to job seekers and focused in the areas that they excel in—opposed to the monolithic coliseum approach by either CareerBuilder or Monster.

Job Board	More Info		POST A JOB
Posted	**Latest Jobs**	**Category**
May 19, 2010	News Bloggers at Indyposted	Blogger
May 18, 2010	Talented Writers Wanted at Demand Studios	Blogger
Jun 01, 2010	Bloggers and Reviewers Wanted at Bizpocket	Blogger
May 31, 2010	Entrepreneurial Writers Wanted at AnyClip Startup Summer program	Blogger
May 31, 2010	Looking for an experienced writer for interview at Fortune 500 CEO	Blogger
May 30, 2010	Web Hosting Reviewer at Keenways Solutions	Blogger
May 29, 2010	Android Apps Blogger at Android-Apps.com	Blogger
May 28, 2010	Content Editor at The Burros	Blogger
May 28, 2010	Financial Markets Blogger at Hidden Pivot Enterprises	Blogger
May 27, 2010	Mobile Tech Blogger / Editor at IntoMobile	Blogger

Corporate blogging software

As you already know, installing and maintaining a basic WordPress site is pretty simple. However, companies that don't have a technical resource have NO idea how it works, nor how to get it up and running. This is where you and your knowledge of this awesome platform come flying in to save the day.

For smaller companies, you can easily charge $1,000 to set up a WordPress-powered site on their own GoDaddy hosting account (around $10 a month). For larger corporations, setting up a blogging platform with the proper workflows can easily fetch $500 to $1000 a month.

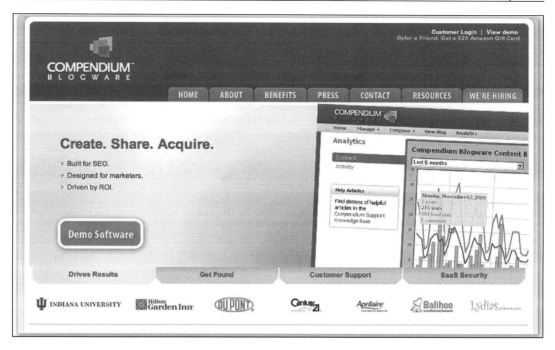

Compendium Blogware is a provider of "Enterprise Blog hosting", and while they don't use WordPress, they do charge a significant amount of money to help to train, and by offering training and support. I can promise you that in your home town, one of the bigger companies is trying to figure out their "blogging" strategy right now. They need your help, and they would be willing to spend $1000 a month to get it. Just make sure you tell them that Brandon sent you.

Hosting WordPress

Why not start a WordPress cloud hosting service? The market is huge and only a few web-hosting companies have figured out that hosting is about the applications and not about the hardware. Using the power of Amazon EC2 or RackspaceCloud, you can easily bring up "virtual" servers with WordPress (even a customized version of WordPress with your brand).

`Site5.com` has this figured out; they offer WordPress-specific hosting and have even contributed a handful of themes to the open source community. As the momentum of WordPress continues, more and more non-technical people will start wanting the flexibility and manageability of WordPress. The first thing these people will search for is "How to start a WordPress blog".

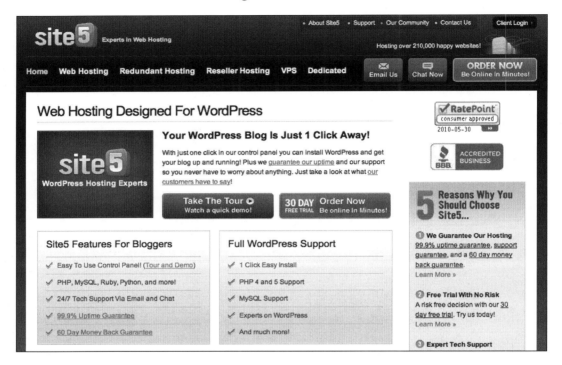

Continuing education

WordPress changes fast, and to become a true student, one must continually learn and evolve their understanding of what WordPress is and can ultimately be. Luckily, there are plenty of resources online to help keep you up-to-date on the latest and greatest in the WP Universe.

- **WordPress Plugin Directory** (`http://wordpress.org/extend/plugins`) is the official directory of Free WordPress plugins.

- **Smashing Magazine** (`http://smashingmagazine.com`) is an online magazine focused on design and web development. Smashing also often commissions designers and developers to create free WordPress themes and plugins.

- **Nettuts+** (http://net.tutsplus.com), like Smashing, offers tons of great articles covering WordPress, plugins, and web development in general.

- **WPPlugins.com** (http://wpplugins.com) is, according to their slogan, the WordPress App Store. They sell premium WordPress plugins that are not available in the free directory.

- **Delicious** (http://delicious.com/popular/wordpress) is continually updated with the latest and most popular posts about WordPress from the entire blogosphere.

- **WooThemes** (http://woothemes.com) is one of today's hottest WordPress design firms. In addition to selling beautiful themes, they also offer a handful of stunning free themes.

- **ChangingWay** (http://changingway.org/) is Andrew Watson's personal, but awesome, blog that frequently covers WordPress and other web topics.

Summary

WordPress, its plugins, and its developer community makes for one incredible platform, which if handled properly, could create a profitable and powerful business. I sincerely hope that you can take a few of the plugins and ideas that I have presented in this book to create something amazing, something that hopefully could free you to work for yourself and make some real changes in the world.

In this chapter, we covered:

- Prototyping with WordPress
- How real business models can run on WordPress
- Making money selling themes, plugins, and digital goods
- Offering job boards, WordPress hosting, and corporate blogging software
- Additional resources to learn more about WordPress and WordPress Plugins

Index

URL 108
CRON job 40
CSS 19

D

digital product
  adding 137
  categories 137
  price and stock control 138
  product detail 137
  product downloading 140
  product images 139
  shipping details 138, 139
  tags 138
Donation Can plugin
  about 124
  Administrator Dashboard widget 124
  manual install URL 124

E

e-mail ideas, Email Users
  exclusive emailer 206
  helping a cause 206
  special deals and promotions 206
Edit Flow plugin
  about 155, 156
  manual install URL 156
Email Users
  about 204, 205
  e-mail ideas 205
  manual install URL 205
Error Reporting
  about 188, 189
  auto delete 189
  configuration 189
  manual install URL 188
Exec-PHP plugin
  about 97, 98
  latest tweets, listing 98
  manual install URL 98

F

Facebook 119
Favicons plugin
  about 88-90

Gravatar icon, using as Favicon 91
  manual install URL 89
  picking, from gallery 90
  remote icon, using 91
  setting up 90
features, BuddyPress. *See* **BuddyPress features**
feed, burning
  blog feed URL, verifying 63
  feed, adding 63
  feed, naming 64
  Google account, creating 63
Feedburner Feedsmith plugin
  about 62
  feed, burning 63
  manual install URL 62
  WP-Feedburner, configuring 64
Fluency Admin
  about 192
  login screen, styling 193, 194
  manual install URL 192
  quick key access 193
forums, BuddyPress 106

G

GD Star Rating plugin
  about 23, 24
  default ratings, fixing 24
  manual install URL 24
Gizmodo 219
Google AdSense 129
Google AdSense Ad
  adding, to Advertising Manager 132
  creating 130, 131
Google AdWords 120
Gravatar 91
Group Documents, BuddyPress plugins
  about 111, 112
  manual install URL 111
groups, BuddyPress 106
Guest Blogger plugin
  about 159, 160
  manual install URL 160
  new article import, adding 160

N

NextGen Gallery plugin
about 30
gallery, adding to post or page 32
gallery, setting up 31
manual install URL 30

O

open source business model 215
options, Sociable plugin
alpha mask on share toolbar, disabling 71
Awe.sm account 72
image directory 72
open in new window option 72
sprite usage for images, disabling 71
tagline 71
toolbar positions 71
use text links 72
use Thisbox/iFrame on links option 72

P

PHP references 19
Plugin Editor 21
plugins, WordPress. *See* **WordPress plugins**
plugins update
CSS 19
JavaScript 20
PHP references 19
tinkering 19
WordPress plugin API 19
plugin supports control , WP-CMS Post Control plugin
page controls 159
post controls 159
Post Layout plugin
about 94, 95
content, inserting 95, 96
manual install URL 94
Pre-Publish Reminder plugin
about 154, 155
manual install URL 155
Private Messages for WordPress plugin
about 167
manual install URL 167

profiles, BuddyPress 105
Prowl 86, 88

Q

Quick Cache
about 186
manual install URL 186
Quick Cache options
about 187
cache expiration time 187
client-side cache 187
dynamic cache pruning 187
get request 187
internal debugging 187
logged in users 187
MD5 Version Salt 188
mutex file locking 188
no-cache referrer patterns 187
no-cache URL patterns 187
no-cache user-agent patterns 187
Quick Cache ON/OFF 187

R

real business models, with WordPress
about 216
advertising spots, selling 219
corporate blogging software 220, 221
digital goods, selling 216, 217
job board 220
plugins, selling 218
themes, selling 217
WordPress, hosting 221
Recent Comments plugin
about 27, 28
manual install URL 28
Redirection
about 212
manual install URL 212
repair 182
resources, WordPress plugins
ChangingWay 223
Delicious 223
Nettuts+ 223
Smashing Magazine 222
WooThemes 223

Thank you for buying
WordPress Top Plugins

About Packt Publishing

Packt, pronounced 'packed', published its first book "*Mastering phpMyAdmin for Effective MySQL Management*" in April 2004 and subsequently continued to specialize in publishing highly focused books on specific technologies and solutions.

Our books and publications share the experiences of your fellow IT professionals in adapting and customizing today's systems, applications, and frameworks. Our solution based books give you the knowledge and power to customize the software and technologies you're using to get the job done. Packt books are more specific and less general than the IT books you have seen in the past. Our unique business model allows us to bring you more focused information, giving you more of what you need to know, and less of what you don't.

Packt is a modern, yet unique publishing company, which focuses on producing quality, cutting-edge books for communities of developers, administrators, and newbies alike. For more information, please visit our website: www.packtpub.com.

About Packt Open Source

In 2010, Packt launched two new brands, Packt Open Source and Packt Enterprise, in order to continue its focus on specialization. This book is part of the Packt Open Source brand, home to books published on software built around Open Source licences, and offering information to anybody from advanced developers to budding web designers. The Open Source brand also runs Packt's Open Source Royalty Scheme, by which Packt gives a royalty to each Open Source project about whose software a book is sold.

Writing for Packt

We welcome all inquiries from people who are interested in authoring. Book proposals should be sent to author@packtpub.com. If your book idea is still at an early stage and you would like to discuss it first before writing a formal book proposal, contact us; one of our commissioning editors will get in touch with you.

We're not just looking for published authors; if you have strong technical skills but no writing experience, our experienced editors can help you develop a writing career, or simply get some additional reward for your expertise.

WordPress Plugin Development: Beginner's Guide

ISBN: 978-1-847193-59-9   Paperback: 296 pages

Build powerful, interactive plug-ins for your blog and to share online

1. Everything you need to create and distribute your own plug-ins following WordPress coding standards

2. Walk through the development of six complete, feature-rich, real-world plug-ins that are being used by thousands of WP users

3. Written by Vladimir Prelovac, WordPress expert and developer of WordPress plug-ins such as Smart YouTube and Plugin Central

WordPress 3 Site Blueprints

ISBN: 978-1-847199-36-2   Paperback: 300 pages

Ready-made plans for 9 different professional WordPress sites

1. Everything you need to build a varied collection of feature-rich customized WordPress websites for yourself

2. Transform a static website into a dynamic WordPress blog

3. In-depth coverage of several WordPress themes and plugins

4. Packed with screenshots and step-by-step instructions to help you complete each site

Please check **www.PacktPub.com** for information on our titles

WordPress and Flash 10x Cookbook

ISBN: 978-1-847198-82-2   Paperback: 268 pages

Over 50 simple but incredibly effective recipes to take control of dynamic Flash content in Wordpress

1. Learn how to make your WordPress blog or website stand out with Flash

2. Embed, encode, and distribute your video content in your Wordpress site or blog

3. Build your own .swf files using various plugins

4. Develop your own Flash audio player using audio and podcasting plugins

WordPress for Business Bloggers

ISBN: 978-1-847195-32-6   Paperback: 356 pages

Promote and grow your WordPress blog with advanced plug-ins, analytics, advertising, and SEO

1. Gain a competitive advantage with a well polished WordPress business blog

2. Develop and transform your blog with strategic goals

3. Create your own custom design using the Sandbox theme

4. Apply SEO (search engine optimization) to your blo

Please check **www.PacktPub.com** for information on our titles

Printed in Great Britain
by Amazon.co.uk, Ltd.,
Marston Gate.